# EMBODIED

## PRAISE FOR *EMBODIED*

"Swami Jaya Devi—who has been my spiritual teacher for 15 years—offers words that are a balm for my heart and a reminder for why the practices of yoga and meditation are essential for me to continue to show up in the world as a Black yogi, scholar, and advocate for justice.

—Chelsea Jackson Roberts, PhD, internationally celebrated Peloton yoga teacher and social justice activist

"Swami Jaya Devi's work literally saved my life. I could not have approached, much less surrendered to it, if this teacher and her community had not been authentically intersectional, and fiercely committed to social justice. Whoever you are: you are welcome and valued in these pages, exactly as you are, and in them you will find the tools of love that will help you heal yourself and our world."

—Scott Turner Schofield, actor, producer, transgender activist

"A heartfelt reminder that yoga is a way of relating – not just to ourselves, but to each other and the world."

—Daniel Simpson, author of *The Truth of Yoga*

"With raw vulnerability, humor and power, Swami Jaya Devi shares her journey – inspired by an ancient toolkit – to finding love in the most impossible situations. Swami challenges each of us to use all of life as fuel, to stand boldly at the eye of what appears as life's storms, and through all of it, to love anyway."

—Dr. Sue Morter, #1 best-selling author of *The Energy Codes* and founder of The Morter Institute for BioEnergetics. www.DrSueMorter.com

"Swami Jaya Devi bases each of her ten chapters on one of the *yamas* and *niyamas*, the principles of restraint and positive observance laid out long ago in Patanjali's classic *Yogasutra*. She explores these ancient teachings not only as universal truths, but also as the inborn means we can apply in dealing with the unique challenges of our modern technological age. Jaya Devi recalls incidents from her own life that range from the daily humdrum to the exceptional stand-out moments, all compellingly told. The author is eager to show how yoga, as a way of life, can transform every moment into an experience of inner and outer harmony, an experience of peace and unity through which we embrace all beings in selfless love, at once bettering ourselves and reaching out to a world in need of healing."

—Devadatta Kali, author of *Managing the Mind: A Commonsense Guide to Patanjali's Yogasutra*

# EMBODIED

An Urban Yogi's Memoir +
Manifesto for Modern Living

SWAMI JAYA DEVI

NEW DEGREE PRESS

COPYRIGHT © 2022 SWAMI JAYA DEVI

EMBODIED

*An Urban Yogi's Memoir + Manifesto for Modern Living*

ISBN    979-8-88504-902-3 *Paperback*
       979-8-88504-903-0 *Kindle Ebook*
       979-8-88504-904-7 *Ebook*

*For my sisters, who taught me how to love.*

*For my students, who live these teachings every day.*

*For my guru, who showed me that
there are no throwaway people.*

# CONTENTS

# PREFACE

## There Are No Throwaway People

COVID-19 is my second pandemic. I was a wide-eyed, twenty-something, newly minted yoga teacher the first time a mysterious disease rocked my sense of security and taught me the unnerving lessons of impermanence. I had recently graduated from college with a fine arts degree and was steeped in midtown Atlanta's blossoming art scene. It was the mid-1980s, and I loved hanging out and making art with a wildly creative, eclectic crowd. All of us were exploring who we were through any kind of self-expression—art, gender, music, writing—that revealed authenticity and truth. We were all pushing against social norms that didn't fit us, wanting something more raw, unique, and real. The relentless fire of the AIDS epidemic had begun raging, escorting gender identity and sexual orientation out of the closet and into homes and hospitals across the nation. A number of fellow artists were grappling with the bias of that time, struggling to live authentically as lesbian, gay, bisexual, transgender, and queer (LGBTQ) people.

When a couple of friends got sick—really sick—I showed up for them in any way I could. I was deep into my exploration of yoga and meditation, getting fully present and blissed-out, and thought the methods I was learning might help: how to observe your emotions and reactions rather than jumping into their chaos, how to use your breath to come back to center, how to touch into okayness, even when nothing is okay. I didn't think these practices were a cure for anything, but I thought they could help these young, outlandish, soul-searching individuals who were afraid of dying.

I started teaching free contemplative arts, yoga, and meditation classes for AIDS and HIV+ at Grady, Atlanta's big inner-city hospital. People invited friends and it grew. I took courses on AIDS to learn what I could, but no one really understood what was happening yet—just that an infectious disease was spreading fast, caught mostly by gay men, needle users, and sex workers. And all of them were showing up in my classes.

*We would come together in a disarray of heartache, fear, opinion, and confusion, do yoga, meditate, and leave a little more okay.*

We would come together in a disarray of heartache, fear, opinion, and confusion, do yoga, meditate, and leave a little more okay. We were longing for meaning and searching for the sacred connection that underlies all of life. The cohesion of practice touched us all, weaving together a community of outcasts, a bond of marginalization.

Enrolled in my third teacher training, I asked every adept or senior yogi I could find how to teach people living with AIDS. No one had an answer. No one was really that interested. Most teachers were into the poses, the flexibility, the bendy body stuff. I was into the experience, the high, the peace, the closeness created. So I just kept learning, working on healing my own suffering and sharing the teachings with people I loved.

Then I heard a celebrated yogi and AIDS activist speak at a celebration deep in the Jemez Mountains of northern New Mexico. Ma Jaya was receiving the "Woman of Peace" award, dressed in vibrant scarlet red with gold bangles clattering on her wrists and a slash of black hair draped across sun-browned skin. Standing in stark contrast to the sea of yogis all dressed in ethereal white, Ma spoke of her work with marginalized communities. You could feel her realness, her caring, and her heartache.

In her thick Brooklyn accent, she simply said, "There are no throwaway people."

As this truth echoed out across the hot, silent, cross-legged crowd, I thought, *Ahh, there it is: inarguable truth.* Her words blazed into me, touching a core belief that we all deserve to be happy, that none of us is expendable.

Learning to stand in the eye of the storm of the AIDS epidemic altered the course of my life. It taught me to be relentlessly present with my heart and eyes open. I didn't know how to change the trajectory of anyone's life, but I showed up and assisted countless people through their deaths, loving them through all of it. It's what I would have wanted: someone terrified right next to me, looking death in the eye and telling me it would be okay.

*It's what I would have wanted: someone terrified right next to me, looking death in the eye and telling me it would be okay.*

This is when I began to understand the power of radical love—love that is lived—that invokes compassionate, intentional presence. This love bears witness with acceptance and kindness. It teaches us to embody an expansive disposition that lifts us all to our highest self. *Yoga* means union: to make whole, to unite and stand daringly open with whatever life hands you, to choose love over fear, especially when it seems impossible. These folks taught me, as I taught them—we taught each other together—how to die a conscious death. This taught us all to be outrageously present and to lean in and live an openhearted life.

These potent skills carried me through the AIDS epidemic and refined me through decades of teaching and practicing. I became an urban yoga monk, devoting my time, love, and energy to helping people find themselves and their inner truths. By opening Atlanta's only urban yoga ashram, I focused on using meditation, breathwork, and yoga to empower people on their path to being more fully themselves. I also started a karma yoga program—putting loving kindness into action by feeding people on the streets, helping kids in the hospitals, and teaching meditation and yoga in the prisons—because working with marginalized communities feels like an embodiment of love. However, my second pandemic is startlingly similar to the first: it is a global health crisis that is peeling back the skin of raging social inequality. The world is not well, and we need tools for wellness that are relevant, accessible, and powerful.

Can the tools of mindful awareness mitigate some of the damage? Can they instigate revolutionary healing? If we are brave enough to do real inner labor—uprooting what no longer works and practicing what does—can these contemplative arts teach us the skills to put wholeness into action?

If there are no throwaway people, can each of us heal ourselves with authenticity and uniqueness and begin to heal the world? The answer, I believe, is yes. It is why I am writing this book.

## Diversity, Inclusivity, and Cultural Appropriation

In a recent conversation with Susanna Barkataki, yoga-activist and author of *Embrace Yoga's Roots*, she queried, "Can you celebrate and share another culture's wisdom without stealing it?"

As a white woman who has lived and practiced yoga in the US for over forty years and has been ordained as a *swami*—a revered teacher—I am aware of cultural appropriation, which is the unacknowledged or inappropriate taking of another culture's customs or practices, usually by a privileged, dominant society. My tradition, along with many other Western yoga traditions, has roots in India that we honor, but we are white people benefiting from an indigenous practice. Because of this, I return to Barkataki's question often, both in my own practice and in my teaching and leadership role as spiritual director of a nonprofit yoga ashram. The question has become a kind of *mantra*—a tool of awareness—that informs and influences me. I hope to never stop investigating or learning from new information and perspectives, and to remember that there is no "perfect." There is only practice.

Here is my response to the question now:

The Western, body-centric approach to yoga is a narrow one, focusing too much on the body, not enough on the expansive happiness and well-being that a full practice can instigate. According to yogic philosophy and texts, these techniques are intended for everyone, of all body types and abilities, because yoga is not about your deepest backbend, it's about your deepest life. The true stretch of yoga is the stretch of living with compassion and integrity. It stretches us to embody outrageous love. It asks us to make the mindfulness tools of yoga accessible to everyone. In a time of great upheaval, we—and the world—need these empowering practices more than ever.

We can honor yoga's roots by teaching its completeness, including its rich Indian heritage, and we can do that without romanticizing or misappropriating that culture. We can draw upon ancient traditions with respect for their ability to transform our daily, modern lives.

We can realize that these practices contain a powerful outline for social justice.

If we pledge to consciously address cultural appropriation in yoga, we—searchers, seekers, lovers of yoga—will find it together. An genuine practice can be studied and respected for the power it creates—the power to bring us all into wholeness as, collectively, we create a more just and loving world.

# INTRODUCTION
# UNLEARNING YOURSELF INTO BEING

*"Yoga is the journey of the self, through the self, to the self."*

## The Lies That Bind Us

Violet—a regular in my weekly meditation class—is visibly distraught, bellowing herself into a full-throttle crisis. She and her boyfriend are meeting with me to discuss her anxiety around their impending nuptials. Hands shaking, breath huffing, she vehemently exclaims, "I am coming unglued." Her fiancé, Ray, is standing to one side in the room with us, obviously in love, but watching her drama unfold. He leans casually against the wall, arms crossed thoughtfully over his chest. He speaks softly out of the corner of his mouth, a tiny smirk on his full lips.

"Because you are glued up all wrong," he acknowledges with gentleness and hint of sly humor. They look across the room at each other, an entire dialogue in one glance. She, defending her unraveling stance. Him, open, loving her but curious to whatever was about to ensue.

She snorts and begins laughing and crying at the exact same time, a raw surge of emotion erupting from within. She is unlearning—letting go of a false belief—that she does not really deserve this kind, loving man, that she is not worthy of this type of partner and mate. In the release, she is healing in real time.

## The Great Unlearning

All of us have places where we are glued together wrong—where we have bought into traditions, belief systems, habits, addictions, or unconscious behaviors that don't reflect who we are. We must unlearn our way back to the most true version of ourselves, so we can really be us and be free. Through this process, we unshackle ourselves. We peel back what is false to reveal what is real. This is true yoga—the great unlearning—which, in turn, reveals our greatness. We learn who we are by untangling ourselves from who we are not.

The first step is to acknowledge that we are ever-evolving works in progress—and always will be. We are not our anger. We are not our unworthiness. We are not even our accomplishments. We can let go of these false beliefs and in the process be fully human: wounded, flawed, messy, kind, and honest. We can use life-affirming practices to regain equanimity while we explore radical freedom. All of us want to live spaciously—with ourselves and all our complexities—as we embrace, connect, and interact with everyone else.

## Calling Your Voice into Being

No one else can do the work of deep inner healing for me. No one else can do it for you. I have worked to develop a true, resonant voice over decades of teaching, sharing, and learning to speak truth with kindness and want to share tools and practices so you can too. This work, grounded in the philosophical teachings of yoga, enhances and strengthens my relationship to myself—not to my egoic self, my lower, needy mind, but to my higher self, the one who loves to love.

If I want a clear voice, I must hone it. I must shatter any habitual silence and heal any habitual rage to unmute and empower myself. In this, I become a catalyst and change-maker. Even amid the chaos of modern life, any of us can willingly pursue our inner work to transform our relationship with our wounds. All of us must find our singular clear voice and holler ourselves out of our history and into intentional joy.

## Ten Tools for Transformation

This book contains a toolkit that anyone can use. It presents a set of teachings, accompanied by practices, that we can utilize to resolve internal aggression, move through pain into empowerment, and embody real wisdom. The ten tools are based in classical yoga philosophy and are exemplified through my own story: overcoming my precarious past, using suffering as fuel to grow, and creating a life brimming with integrity, love, and freedom. Here, yoga's ageless wisdom is filtered through my modern-day experience—because yoga is meant to be lived.

These tools for transformation radically changed my life from being woefully unworthy to being happy with simply being me, to being an empowered spiritual warrior that uses wisdom tools to help the world. They taught me to embody self-worth. For forty years, I explored, experimented with, experienced, and extrapolated these teachings, and this book is born of that effort. I've watched these methods refine and inspire thousands of people's lives and I want them to do this for you as well.

First, we investigate five tools of unlearning—to release habits that no longer serve us. In *Patanjali's Yoga Sutra,* these are called the *yamas,* or restraints, and here I interpret them through a modern, relevant lens.

Then we have a second set of five tools that teach us the art of becoming—becoming more authentically us. These are the *niyamas,* the yogi's tools of empowerment.

As we dive into this work together, ask:

- What am I ready to heal or transform?

- How free, empowered, and happy do I want to be?

- Which of these tools appeals to me?

- Which practice will I choose first?

If you want a fresh take on using ancient tools to create yourself into the expansive existence you genuinely want to live, then this is the book for you. The tools in this book can be used in any order, to address any situation. They can help you identify, claim, and become your truest self.

These are the tools that shook me down, taught me who I am, lit me up, then sent me soaring.

Enter into the wild wisdom experience of real transformation with me using ten timeless empowerment techniques to create a life that is openhearted, joyful, and satisfying.

# 1
# RESOLVING INTERNAL AGGRESSION

**Ahimsa:** (uh-HIM-suh) nonviolence; non-harming

*"Nonviolence is absolute commitment to the way of love."*

DR. MARTIN LUTHER KING, JR.

## The Aura of Kali and the Eggs of Rage

Squeezing through the crowded meditation hall, I plopped my fat, crescent-shaped cushion down onto the dark floor near the back wall, far from the teaching platform at the front of the room. The effulgent Dattatreya Temple was spilling over with devotees, the room humming around me. I nestled my spine against the base of a huge statue of a wild, Black wisdom goddess. Glancing up over my shoulder, I beheld the towering figure of Kali, the goddess of equity and destroyer of illusion.

I was attending my first meditation retreat at Sacred Kashi, Ma Jaya's interfaith yoga ashram in south central Florida. Yoga lays out a spiritual path that aspires to honor all and exclude none. Here, the high-ceilinged room was reverently adorned with sacred statuary from many of the world's faith traditions: a long-haired Christ in flowing robes stood regally next to a rotund, pink, elephant-headed Ganesh, the Hindu remover of obstacles. A gold *Avalokiteshvara*, the buddha of compassion, was encircled by a halo of one thousand shining arms with a painted blue Tibetan eye centered in the palm of each hand. A finely crafted Native American dreamcatcher hung resplendent beside an ornate Jewish menorah. Spiritual paintings and icons representing yoga's inclusive interfaith tradition were respectfully placed and cared for, all gleaming in the slanted, tropical afternoon sun.

Every day, for hours on end, I sat in meditation, listening and absorbing, snug against the feet of Kali's life-size form. The goddess Kali represents radical, revolutionary awakening. Another translation of her Sanskrit name is reality—stark, unadorned reality—symbolized by her nakedness and her garland of flowers entwined with skulls. Each of us experiences the beauty of life and the heartbreak of death, and Kali's image portrays that mystical reality. The tantric goddesses are archetypes of wisdom, representing sacred energies that we can work with on our quest for healing. Kali embodies transformation, which is often intense because it is your illusions, desires, and attachments, as well as your aversions and fears that will be revealed to be transformed. I was unfamiliar with Kali until that moment, but she was about to change my perspective on yoga and the courage it takes to truly become whole.

## The Aura of Kali

A few weeks before this encounter with Kali, I was attending an art event in Atlanta, my hometown. Standing in the sparkling gallery, I gazed steadily at a large, lush painting, as a tall auburn-haired woman approached and perched next to me, carefully observing the same work of art. We began to chat, admiring the artwork, then bonded over this powerful abstract painting that was shimmering with expression, rich with a vibrant impasto force. Dr. Ariel Grace and I clicked immediately. Our conversation flowed effortlessly from art and self-expression to meditation and unorthodox spirituality.

Ariel is an artist, Jungian psychologist, devotee of the Indian guru Sri Aurobindo, and psychic aura reader. I immediately signed up for an aura reading with her—how could I not? She was a gifted healer and an extraordinary human being. She and I became allies as she helped me heal using unconventional, creative methods. I felt that I had just found my guru in Ma Jaya, but now I had found a teacher and mentor to help me understand what having a guru meant. I was having many unsettling experiences with my own energy body as *kundalini*, the energy of awareness, was igniting. So I thought someone reading my energy field was a good idea. Having just returned from Ma's immersive meditation intensive, I was feeling deeply rearranged but happy about my scheduled reading with Ariel.

Ariel's office was in a nondescript gray building surrounded by woods and tall leafy trees. Her space was clean, plain, even austere, but I felt at home immediately, in the way you do in a space that somehow welcomes you. It wasn't a space that told you how to be, it was more blank canvas, asking who you are. As we walked further into the space we would be working in, there was a comfy couch and deep chair to accommodate us.

She welcomed me in. We took off our shoes and settled into a short, simple meditation. It felt like a spiritual handshake, a getting to know one another, eyes twinkling at the end.

Then, with what felt like very little instruction, she left me alone in a room filled with art supplies. Fun! Intimidating, but fun. Running my hands over a rainbow tray of chalky pastel crayons, I chose orange, hot pink, dusky green. In big sweeping arcs, I began to draw, scraping the rough-smooth texture of the chalk against the grainy newsprint. With a comforting crayon smell infusing the space, I spent the next ten minutes sketching an intuitive drawing. I wasn't really sure what I was supposed to be doing, but simply went with it because it was joyful and creative, and I already trusted her. The instructions were to create an abstract drawing of how I was feeling. I was loving it, and the images flew from my hands. I like to draw with my whole body moving—just feeling and expressing, not overthinking or trying to impress—following color, shape, and mood. I wished the paper was bigger; there was so much to feel, so much content, so much ready to be revealed.

As I took a step back, tilting my head to one side to observe my work, Ariel strode back into the room. My bold drawing was there on display on a spindly wooden easel between us. She ignored the illustration completely and we sat down, face to face, me at one end of the puffy couch, her on the single chair. She stared at and through me for three or four solid minutes, which felt like a lifetime. Just looking intently at me, sparkly eyed and breathing deep breaths. I started feeling humbly exposed and resoundingly seen.

She blinked her big blue eyes slowly, took a full breath and said, "There is a wildly intense image imprinted into your aura, and I don't know that I've ever seen anything like this before. I'm taken aback. This is a new experience for me. I'm sure you came with questions and ideas but there is no disputing that this is what we will need to talk about. We are in uncharted territory; I believe, for both of us."

We paused and both took deep breaths.

"There is a huge Black goddess, almost like an African spider goddess, with multiple arms and legs vibrating in your energy field. She is so powerfully dominant I am almost speechless. I can't decide if I should bow down or run from the room."

*There is a huge Black goddess with multiple arms and legs vibrating in your energy field. She is so powerfully dominant, I am almost speechless. I can't decide whether to bow down or run from the room.*

This was not what I expected her to say. Recalling that the tantric goddess Kali—who I had just encountered—is midnight black and dances with her many arms spinning recklessly about her, I timidly mentioned her name. Ariel gasped in wonder and recognition.

"Om Namah Kali!" she cried out—a mantra, honoring the goddess.

Now I felt like running from the room. With my belly and hands quivering, she and I locked eyes. Both of our jaws dropped open as we simultaneously sprung tears, as this moment of startling recognition gave birth to a mystical friendship like none I have had before or since.

## The Eggs of Rage

Soon into the acquaintance, I asked Ariel to guide me in healing my anger with my family. I was raised in a boozy,

Irish Catholic brawl of too many siblings and not enough…
anything. I felt a hot malcontent around this familial brand
of neglect and was ready to unleash some long-standing, sti-
fled emotion so I could get free. I was weary of being shackled
to the pain of the past, but uncertain how to release it without
harming anyone. With older brothers who felt entitled to lay
hands where hands should not go, it was time to discharge
the cellular burden of family shame. Ariel and I set up a
series of sessions that included meditation, intentional calling out, transformative release, and energy cleansing. But
inevitably when the two of us would get together, some kind
of art would happen. As I worked through an onslaught of
repressed anguish, my artistic instincts arose right along
with my indignation.

One night I was journaling at home, unearthing long
buried childhood trauma. Sometimes I feared that if I pulled
hard enough on one thread, I would unravel my own sense of
self until my belonging became a pile of useless knots, bereft
on the floor. This complex tapestry of realization would
untangle down a dark path, leading mostly to despair. How
could my parents turn those bleary blank eyes away from so
much suffering? How could they choose to just not see? The
blindness of the next cocktail, ensuring their safe passage
to the next morning, obliterated any safety for those they
brought into the world. On deep forays like this, investigating
the rough texture, the warp and the weft of old wounding,
journaling often didn't feel like enough. I needed a more
vivid expression than words could hold.

As a yogi, I process things viscerally through my body and
I inevitably enter physically into the memory of experience.
Uncontained by the linear borders of a safe, smooth yoga
mat, I began to practice yoga in the sanctity of my home,

bare hands and feet embracing cold hardwood floors. Moving up and down the central hallway, feeling, crying, twisting, embodying memory to release it. Breathe, don't breathe. Feel, don't feel. Flow into a yoga pose and ask it to teach me. Open into a shape, a frame, a posture as it shows me where to heal. Breathe, don't breathe. Feel, don't feel. Move again, pose by pose until the repression bubbles up my throat. Drop down on my knees, hands together in prayer, bowing slowly backward, lifting my chest, my inner heart to the sky. My head falls back, exposing my throat, and I feel the blockage, the strangle, the hand holding in place the rage of words unspoken. My hurt pours upward on the sound of a chant, a heartbroken cry, and release. Pose after pose I wring myself out, a panting animal form slathered slick in sweat, tears dripping from my face.

Rage was a demon and I slowly, intentionally raised my head and invited her in. I wanted the hurt to move out of me, to dislodge it from my body. I wanted to throw things, to push it out, to embody this rage and destroy something. I wanted to call up the face of every single family member and then burn them to the ground. I paced around my house. I ranted at the sky. I was swirling in an uncontrollable maelstrom of memory and emotion. I spun in a circle in the center of my home, pivoting, and was suddenly slammed into the center of it all. The silence was shocking. The stillness so abrupt. I stood in the eye of my own transformation, my own healing storm. I was shaking, but I was seeing, feeling, and opening. In destroying the framework of the past, I was cracked open into the present. I collapsed in front of my altar, my sacred meditation space. I got quiet. I listened. I listened inside myself so I could really hear what I was trying to say.

*I got quiet. I listened.*

*I listened inside myself so I could really hear*

*what I was trying to say.*

In the quiet, I was inspired by the power of what I was feeling, the sheer intensity of it all. It was awe inspiring because it was so big, so bestial and terrifying. I was unleashing a torrent of hurt and rage that was both horrifying and exhilarating. In response, I opened and allowed myself to feel all of it until I became settled and spacious. I held my own grief and anger. Then I slowly began to lean into the inspiration behind the torrent.

Where were these feelings coming from? How deep did they go? I was distressed at my riotously neglectful childhood, but what happened if I went underneath the events of my suffering? Could I look beyond my experiences, beyond the events into the raw material? Where was the original suffering?

After a few more moments of quiet introspection, I rose from the meditation cushion. I entered my kitchen and opened my refrigerator.

This is dangerous ground, because most of us are familiar with eating our feelings and numbing out, and the chocolate was right there calling my name. But I was too awake now to go back to sleep. I was looking for a vehicle to express not repress. So, I pulled out a dozen eggs.

I did not make an omelet. I wanted to destroy something, and the eggs spoke to me. They are little symbols of creation of the elemental beginning, and I was drawn to their ironic contrast in my rampage of destruction. I pulled out paints and paintbrushes and started to create a portrait of each one of my ten family members, painted upon an egg.

Eggs are notoriously delicate, so I went from thrashing about with uncontrollable rage coursing through my veins to quietly, intently painting the face of each of my seven siblings and both of my parents. I painted for hours. I painted until the sun began to lighten the eastern sky. I painted tiny details with tiny brushes, infusing each egg portrait with a vibrant persona. I used the energy of hate-filled destruction to create something intricate, delicate, and beautiful. I crafted exquisite, jewel-like works of art, until they shone with personality and insight.

They did not last long in this world.

Sleep deprived but deeply attuned, I straggled in to meet Ariel, carton of eggs tucked safely under one arm.

"What have we here?" Ariel intoned as I opened the box. She sucked in an astonished breath. As I explained my process and my intention, tears welled up in her eyes. She, like me, understood how destruction can be the birthplace of creation.

"Now I need a place to destroy them," I firmly stated.

She begged to be allowed to take photographs, but I declined.

Yes, they were special. They were gorgeous. They were magical little depictions of each individual I had grown up with: those who had laid their hands on me, and those who had held me through the suffering. This is the kind of creation that is born of transcendence, like the Tibetan mandalas made up of sand or the Italian chalk drawings covering the streets and sidewalks of Florence. They are created to illustrate something and then to release it. These works of art embody the impermanent nature of all things, including beauty and tragedy—and we must complete the cycle.

Together, we wandered out into her tree-shaded parking lot and found a peeling, cerulean blue cinderblock wall next to a dark green dumpster. The crumbling structure was facing the woods and seemed to rise straight up out of the dirt, creating the perfect tableau.

I carefully handed the carton to my beloved friend, who gazed into my eyes and slowly, reluctantly opened the lid.

Biting one lip, Ariel whispered, "Pandora's box, for sure."

I lifted my first sibling egg and felt the weight of that cool, smooth surface against my hand. I clutched it against my heart and prayed for healing. I prayed for karmic resolution for all of us. I asked to be released from resentment, anger, aversion, or attachment. I drew back my arm, spring-loaded with tension, and I let that egg fly.

In my best imitation of a baseball pitcher, I hurled egg after egg after egg, heaving out decades of anger and pain, feeling anguish ripple through my body, down my arm and out through each airborne orb. I experienced a visceral release as each ovum took flight, then—splat—eggshell crunching against cinderblock, an embryo ooze dripping thickly down the stone. I grunted with the primal sounds of old trauma departing my body, as the egg siblings landed, one after the other, into a gooey mess of purposeful release. With a final thrust of evisceration, the last egg exploded and my whole family was splattered, in splendor and in shame, across that dappled wall. I sensed the emptiness in my body where torment had once lived.

With an inhale of deep satisfaction, Ariel and I watched the viscous entrails drip, then revolved slowly toward one another. I shivered with the shaky, internal tremors of deep emotional discharge. We hugged, then cried. We screamed, then laughed. We celebrated the letting go. Shucking off the process, but still vibrating with the ritual, I felt light. I was unburdened, liberated from carrying some oppressive weight of family pattern, of ancestral karma. With dead leaves and twigs crunching underfoot, the musky-sweet smell of leaf decay rose. Wiping egg off the side of one cheek, I slipped my hand into hers as we walked back inside.

## Ahimsa: Resolving Internal Aggression

Anger and rage are volatile, action-oriented emotions. They are not passive. They bleed out of us, poisoning our inner and outer environment. The experience of embodied aggression is often so intolerable that the urge to act out physically overtakes our rationality, our values, and our hearts.

The yogic principle of *ahimsa*, or intentional nonviolence, teaches us to understand and courageously examine the root of these primal impulses, so that we are no longer ruled by them. Adopting a nonviolent attitude doesn't mean the rage goes away. It means we change our relationship with our internal aggression. Once we stop thrashing about, trying to get rid of our anger or attempting to offload it onto someone else, we can become curious about how to express powerful, intense feelings with emotional and spiritual presence. Feeling, or trying not to feel, is what anger and rage are really all about. Ironically, that concept angers a lot of people, because they don't want to feel or talk about feelings—both create too much exposure. Anger and rage are often so uncomfortable that we just want to get away from what we feel or move it out of ourselves, so we act.

Even the toughest among us are sensitive, emotional beings, and our volatile sentiments prove that. We don't act enraged unless we are passionate about something—typically something that has hurt us. All of us get wounded, frustrated, and angry, and these are normal human emotions in reaction to normal human experiences. Having a temper tantrum is a sign that there is room for deeper spiritual work ahead. Confronting our anger is the work of real emotional maturity. It takes courage to sit with and open to the feelings of rage. It takes even more bravery to search within and uncover the pain that lurks beneath our reactions.

How can we feel the white-hot strike of being painfully affronted? Rather than retaliate, can we act with integrity? Can we feel our own woundedness and then share what we are feeling with compassion and insight? This is the real stretch of yoga. It takes practice, patience, and perseverance to learn how to do this, to embody compassionate awareness.

Ahimsa, the first of five yamas, is akin to the physicians' Hippocratic oath of "do no harm." The five yamas outlined in *Patanjali's Yoga Sutra*, are the restraints: the things to stop doing, the things that create pain and chaos in our lives, things like anger or rage. Until we overcome violence and aggression, little spiritual growth can occur, because when we do harm, we firmly fix pain into our lives. When we become nonviolent, we don't hit or attack people, get into fistfights, strike our spouse, smack our kids, or kick the dog. We don't engage in physical injury to anyone or even anything. We also don't yell or rage at people. We don't speak with scathing sarcasm or toxic familiarity. We don't flood our bodies with toxic substances or cause intentional self-harm. We restrain ourselves from acts of aggression, observe the impulse to do harm, and instead, make a different choice.

*By taking a personal vow to do no harm,*

*we agree to reach for a consciousness practice,*

*even when we are the most unconscious.*

By taking a personal vow to do no harm, we agree to reach for a consciousness practice, even when we are the most unconscious. We agree to meet our bratty, aggressive nature with compassion, kindness, and presence. We give ourselves a life advantage when we turn toward our inner rage in order to heal it. This powerful step can dramatically change our relationship with ourselves and those around us.

Anger shuts down curiosity, and we lose the capacity to wonder about where the other person is standing. When we can remain inquisitive about another person's experience, we enter empathy and we feel curious about what it is like to live in their shoes.

In a recent chat with Lama Rod Owens, Buddhist teacher, activist, and author of *Love and Rage*, I asked what anger and reactivity could teach us. He shared, "Once you are able to hold anger with spaciousness and not react to it, it can lead you to something much deeper. There is heartbreak under anger—and even more so under rage—and if you're able to touch and share that hurt, real change can happen. You can learn to occupy a space that is much more compassionate, vulnerable, and intimate."

If we can find the inner trigger and share it with authenticity and vulnerability, healing is exponential. When we stop lashing out, our energy changes. The goal is not to stop feeling rage, but to learn to express it in a manner that can heal it instead of causing more harm. When we are daring enough to allow anger to take up space and course through us, yet respond with curiosity and empathy, we can understand and learn from what wounded us. As we do this, we evolve. We make room for love. We expand our ability to live with an open heart. We love anyway.

## The Silence That Costs You

What if you are afraid of expressing anger and avoid conflict at all costs? Rather than cause harm externally or share the vulnerability of feeling hurt, many people hold all that turmoil in. The price of this self-suppression is high. We have a reaction and sequester all that suffering inside, leaving it to smolder in our core. When we are afraid to share our opinion or our woundedness, we not only relinquish our power and voice, but we also harm ourselves. The inability to open and share when we are hurt reinforces self-loathing, depression, disconnection, and unworthiness. It teaches us the ruse of "making nice": pretending that we are okay when we are not. It creates the illusion that we are in control of our pain. When we swallow our true voice, it is a silence that can cost us our peace of mind, our sobriety, our well-being, and even our self-worth.

*Learning how to speak*
*and safely share our anger or suffering*
*is part of the healing journey of ahimsa.*

Learning how to speak and safely share anger or suffering is part of the healing journey of ahimsa. We have to be street smart about this—not putting ourselves in harm's way—which can be more challenging in different social locations. Sometimes the people we are with are not safe, and we must pay wise attention to protect ourselves from someone else's violence.

Also, creating safe spaces doesn't mean we will share our pain perfectly, especially if we have not expressed anger consciously before, but our willingness to be ourselves instead of repressing ourselves is crucial. Our voice is a powerful vehicle of self-healing. When we're hurt and refuse to speak up for ourselves, the violence can happen on the inside. Like a form of self-wounding, this silence can become a habit of inner betrayal that undermines our relationship with ourselves.

It takes subtle discrimination to learn how to be angry and conscious at the same time, to understand that anger does not have to thrust us into regrettable behavior. When angry, we can open and allow ourselves to feel everything, even the awful, heart-rending agony we habitually avoid. In this, we heal. We grow. We begin to discern when it's important to speak and when it's important not to—when to create spaciousness, when to share our inner experience, and when to throw eggs. Ultimately, we want to hone the skills of genuine being: brave enough to handle the world, vulnerable enough to heal from it, and open enough to continue to lovingly embrace it all.

## MINI PRACTICE

### THE BREATH THAT CHANGES EVERYTHING

When you are boiling over with frustration and the acrimony starts to leak out into the atmosphere around you, stop. Hesitate. Breathe. Breathe the deepest breaths of your entire day. Breathe as if your life depends on it. Breathe as if these breaths could save your marriage, your job, or your dignity—because they could.

## Ocean Sounding Breath

*Ujjayi* is the classic yogi's breath whose name means victory. It is used to create full presence. When you pause and breathe during the actual moment as an internal struggle is taking place, you open yourself to the possibility of learning from the experience, rather than being overcome by it. These are some of the most empowering breaths you ever take because the simple act of conscious breathing gives you an opportunity to reach for a higher thought. It creates openness and gives you time and space to feel and be okay with whatever you are feeling.

### Technique

Lengthen and deepen your breath. Begin to make a sighing sound on both the inhale and the exhale. This is like the sound you make when you fog up a mirror, only your lips are closed. Similar to how a scuba diver makes a heavy breath sound while descending into oceanic depths, you make an exaggerated "hhhhh" sound as you inhale and again as you exhale. Keep the sound of the breath at the base of your throat. Use this continuous sound to drop deeper into the experience of the moment, to feel and open, even when the moment is charged with emotion. Continue the breathe until you can do the following self-inquiry.

## Nonviolent Self-Inquiry

Anger is a masquerade to keep us away from a deeper issue. It is a clear symptom of an internal wound. Use this self-inquiry to find the source of the hurt so you can begin the process to reveal and ultimately heal the wounds.

### Technique

Keep doing the breath as you look within yourself, searching beyond the anger or reaction. Answer the following questions:

- What do you experience when you look deeply?
- What is underneath the anger? Is there a subterranean hurt? Can you kindly identify what internal feeling is catalyzing your reaction without blaming anyone?
- Have you been hurt like this before? Is there a pattern of being hurt in a similar manner? Does this hurt remind you of an earlier wound?
- What happens when you give your reaction time and space without judgment, blame, or shame? What happens if you do not push it out or in, but stay present with it?

Write your answers. If and when you are able, discuss your answers with trusted beloveds. Practice speaking about your pain with awareness and compassion. Do your best to have calm, rational, openhearted conversations about what is happening inside you when you are angry and hurt.

# The Bigger Asshole

Words can be violent. We can wound with words almost as much as we can with a physical attack. We can do incredible harm by saying things in frustration, anger, or even ignorance. How do we become mindful of the impact of our words? How do we soften any tendency to lash out in verbal violence?

Anger is a bully and likes to show up for the fight armed with a potent firestorm of brain-melting action. Rather than reveal our pain, we come out swinging. We get hurt, and often in our wounding, we want to hurt the other person back. This is not the easiest thing to look at in ourselves because no one likes to think of themselves as willfully hurting others, but we don't always act as our best selves when we're in pain.

Here, we encounter the astounding phenomenon of being the bigger asshole. Somehow, in our evolutionary history, we decided that if one person in the room is behaving badly, our best choice is to be an even bigger jerk. This is not a very smart strategy when you think about it with detachment, because now two unconscious people are hurling barbs at each other. But in a heated moment, this type of action often seems like an excellent idea. Anger relishes a throwdown. We get hurt, we feel like our beliefs or identity are challenged, and we regress into aggressive cavemen. We try to wound whoever wounded us.

Evolving beyond these clumsy reactions keeps us in touch with our innate humanity. As human beings, we know that we will be hurt in the world. We all experience suffering. We also know that we are brave and inquisitive, able to seek growth, harmony, and healing. In *Untamed*, author and activist Glennon Doyle says, "We can do hard things." We can rise up and say, "Hey, that hurts, let's talk about this," instead of swinging a club.

The real work of ahimsa is to create that gap, that moment of conscious hesitation between us and our instinctive or violent reactions. We learn to pause and feel, open and allow. In that gap lies awareness and power. That gap, the gap of transformation, is where all our growth lies.

## Listening to the Wind

A short distance off the coast in our rugged Cape Cod hometown, my maternal grandmother's hardscrabble backyard was a blustery haven to me, a small child. She would often lean down, place her gnarled hand on my shoulder, and whisper in my ear, "Listen to the wind." As I lifted my head and searched across the flowerbeds, this instruction quieted my mind. I could smell the ocean and feel the buffeting breeze as I learned to pause and open to something bigger, something beyond me. Listening to the wind became a technique to quiet and open my young mind. Later on, when I began to practice meditation in my teens, I keenly felt my grandmother guiding me from beyond to listen, to be present with what is. She lead me to open my field of perception beyond what I know, feel, or think and settle into awareness.

When I am asked to fully listen to someone's pain, I often reference this feeling. Listening to the wind instructs me to listen bigger, to settle down and open up, like grounding and expanding at the same time. Real listening asks me to hold a shared space with reverence and presence. It requires empathy. Empathy asks me to slow down and care enough about another person's experience to really hear them.

Sometimes, when we are focused on sharing our experience, we forget to listen. Effective listening is one-half of effective communication. Clear communication is not just about building our case or explaining why we are right. Creating safe space includes spaciousness for all who are present. Listening for someone else's truth, which may differ from ours, creates the possibility for genuine connection. When we are connected, listening, and caring, the brilliant kindness of who we really are shines.

## MINI PRACTICE

### LISTENING TO THE WIND

This practice can be done anywhere, anytime, with anyone or alone. It's a practice of pausing to create thoughtful presence, like listening to the wind. I use it to connect to my ancestors and their inherited wisdom while connecting to the moment I am in. We use it to connect to wisdom by creating a pause, a gap where we can listen for the deeper essence of our inner heart. You attune yourself to the quiet essence of simple being, so you don't react in harmful ways.

*Technique*
Pause in whatever you are doing. Focus on the sound of your breath—the breath you are breathing in the exact moment of pausing—and hear it like it has become the sound of the wind. Allow the breath to lengthen and deepen. Open to what you feel without judgment or reaction. Just listen to the moment you are living in now. Feel what you feel. Connect to your own aliveness.

## Every Time I Close My Eyes

Shortly after the murder of George Floyd, I was scheduled to give a talk to an advocacy group that uplifts and empowers nonprofit leaders. This session had been scheduled before the COVID-19 pandemic began and had been transferred, like everything else, to an online platform. My contact within the advocacy group was Habib, a young, muscular bearded Black man. I had known him for less than a year, but we had previously enjoyed working together in person at a big conference in Chicago. As we were preparing for the session, Habib and I were checking in, discussing what was occurring in the world around us.

As a yogi, I advocate meditation for all people—all the time. I constantly ask folks how their daily practice is, much to my students' ongoing dismay, because everyone wants to meditate but being consistent with it is challenging.

So, I asked Habib, "How is your practice?"

He took a very big breath. He stared at me through the screen, his dark brown eyes glistening, steadily maintaining a professional stature. Habib is a robust, determined man with a deep, caring heart. He held my gaze and I held his, listening, waiting.

Deliberately choosing his words, he replied, "Swami, every time I close my eyes, all I feel is rage."

He looked at me over the Zoom screen, his countenance brimming over, anger entwined with heartbreak, one clambering over the other. "All I feel is rage."

"Good," I replied. "You should feel rage. Rage is actually a superpower, especially against injustice. And you are a Black man! You should feel rage. But you do have to be wise enough to know how to use it."

Here I sat, a white woman, attempting to mindfully hold this space open with a Black colleague. Feeling the historical reverberation of white women falsely accusing Black men of violence, he and I sat, simply facing each other.

Habib's mouth fell open. He looked at me, shocked and unsettled. He swiped his hand across his face. He said "Damn, Swami. No white person has ever said that to me."

He laughed, wearily.

"Y'all usually back away or try to fix it somehow, gloss over it or make it better. But how the hell am I supposed to use this? My people are being murdered and I cannot tolerate one second of sitting still with it." He spat out that last bit, the sting of hatred for what was being done, what was being tolerated, even condoned. George Floyd had been killed in police custody after passing a counterfeit twenty-dollar bill at a convenience store. A forty-six-year-old Black Minneapolis man, Floyd died after being arrested and held down under the knee of Derek Chauvin, a white police officer subsequently charged and convicted of third-degree murder and second-degree manslaughter (*New York Times*, 2020).

We both listened, together, to his pain echoing across the airwaves. It was big pain—Black pain. It was racial pain rooted in America's shadow history. It was the pain of a marginalized people being held down and suffocated under the boot of white supremacy.

"You could destroy yourself with this rage," I replied, aware of the swirling racial dynamic between us. "You could destroy your own life in a heartbeat. You could destroy your family. You could turn it into addiction. You could go out and protest and burn down the town. You could buy a gun and take out as many people as you could tolerate killing. You could fall effortlessly into the trap that has been set for you. Or you could use it as fuel."

*You could fall effortlessly*

*into the trap the has been set for you.*

*Or you could use it as fuel.*

Habib took a breath. He was obviously engaged in the painful process of exploring the content of his rage with real presence. When we breathe deeply, we feel deeply. When we feel deeply, we become present. We are open to what is happening in the moment, which creates the fuel: the possibility of purposeful choice, the kind of choice that instigates change.

Habib and I reworked the content of the upcoming workshop to this talk, this unbearable reality. This is what America needs to hear, especially the America of nonprofit, grassroots leaders working exhaustively to make a more loving and just world. Remember, Habib was not accustomed to being a presenter. At that time, he was more of a background guy. Yet he was exactly the guy we all needed to hear from: an average Black American man, trying to live a good life. His voice was the relevant voice. He knew that he had something important to say.

Habib generously offered me—and everyone in that workshop—a lens through which to see the world, and it altered me. I'd always believed myself to be a proponent of equality, but my conversation with Habib made clear I could go even further. As I listened to him and attempted to fathom the depth of his pain, I realized how insulated I am, how protected I am by my own white privilege. There was so much more to learn.

One of the attendees of the event was the Black female head of Planned Parenthood, Alexis McGill Johnson. She blew up the chat box with kudos to Habib for his intense presence. He valiantly opened to that difficult conversation, online, in a workshop format, in front of hundreds of powerful community organizers and leaders. Habib used his suffering, and the suffering of his people, as fuel to uplift and inspire others. That is yoga. That is courage, embodied. That is how we show up and live in service to humanity, and to the greater good. It is how we care, deeply, wholeheartedly, one breath, one situation at a time.

## DEEP PRACTICE

### TORRENT OF LOVE MEDITATION

Love is the antidote that heals inner aggression. This holds true for every human being—every gender, race, religion, age, weight, economic, or health status. Even with our wounds and wild range of experiences, we all embody the ability to love and love deeply. We are also smart, creative, and courageous, but we have certain belief systems that we have adopted that are incorrect. These are our mistakes of the intellect.

For instance, we don't believe we are worthy of love, which is a source of great anguish. We think, *"For me to feel loved, you have to love me."* In this, we falsely believe that love only comes from the outside in. We are love. We know how to love. Love is already within us.

The Torrent of Love Meditation disrupts this intellectual mistake. It opens us to an essential possibility: that we are already outrageously loved, we have access to expansive love, and we can use tools to experience and live that love.

*Technique*

Sit in a comfortable meditation position. Close your eyes. Take a few deep breaths. Set an intention to open.

Invite in some energetic assistance, someone you trust. This person should be easy and uncomplicated for you to love. They could be a sibling, friend, partner, or child. They could be a beloved grandparent or pet, living or deceased, but choose someone where love flows easily between you two. No judgment about who it is, just choose where love feels effortless.

Invite them to energetically "sit with you." Pour love into them. Pour it from your heart to theirs. Let it flood through you, holding nothing back. Feel the essence of your inner heart pouring out of your chest in a torrent of love. Just love and love and love. Literally gush love into them in a wave of unbridled love. Open yourself and be bold. Feel all of it. Now, notice how you feel when you let yourself love like this, no holds barred. Notice if you feel loved when you love so freely.

Thank your person or pet for teaching you how to love like this. Then kindly ask them to "depart the practice." See if you can sustain this outpouring of love without them present. Explore the idea that this love is within you, waiting to be set free. Feel this love. Share this love. Be this love. Let love pour through you into the world. Let this love saturate you, so that you never burn out, you never run dry. See everyone through the eyes of love.

In this way, live with the tremendous love of your inner heart silently leading your way.

# 2
# THE TRUEST TRUTH

**Satya:** (SUHT-yah) truth

*"Only the truth of who you are, if realized, will set you free."*

## Behind the Mask of Pretense

It was a sunny, ordinary Tuesday morning when suddenly the attacks of September 11, 2001, began. Over the next few hours, my quiet Atlanta-based mindfulness center was inundated. People poured through our doors for my morning yoga and meditation class, which was occurring during the brutal New York City violence. We breathed and moved, we wept and felt, all while trying to recalibrate and find the ground beneath our unsteady feet.

As this heartbreaking nationwide crisis continued to unfold and the second assault landed in DC, my best friend Judy Martin, a Long Island news anchor, called from the Manhattan streets. She was in shock, clutching the cell phone to her ear, watching as the towers burned, engulfed in a surge of panicked people scattering through the city streets. Judy was lost, shaken, and verging on hysteria. We breathed and cried together. She shared the fear, the intensity, the horror, and the confusion. With her innate reporter's accuracy, she described the experience in excruciating detail: the rain of ash, the misery of public mayhem. She was okay, but her city, her country, and her reality were burning.

The following day, CNN called and asked me to do an interview. They were looking for some insight into how meditation and mindfulness could help a country in crisis. They asked, "How do you address fear with mindfulness? Can yogic tools actually help?"

A few hours later, a news team arrived at our studio, armed with equipment and questions. With a bulky camera hoisted over one shoulder, a slim, ponytailed cameraman wielded an intimidating, glassy eye just to the left of my face. The well-coiffed interviewer, clicking high heels across polished floors, was ready, microphone in hand. I, the barefoot yogi, felt completely out of my comfort zone, even in my own Zen-infused space. Anxiously—I have a lifelong aversion to cameras—I turned toward the reporter. The blinking red light of the looming machine clicked on, and the reporter listed my credentials as the interview began.

She was serious and self-assured, emanating just the right tone of inquisitive hope, and wow, she was making me sound good. Especially the part about leading a Princeton study on meditation, which I had never done. *Holy shit*. I have never been to Princeton, never led a study on mediation in any academic setting whatsoever. I started quietly freaking out. I could feel the gap between who I was and who I was perceived to be opening up, like a roiling chasm of shame.

I was incredibly tempted to pretend to be the person she presented. She was making me sound so smart, so worthy of sharing my vast, research-backed knowledge. Why would I disagree with her? My hands started shaking, palms sweating, heart racing. I took a few tremulous breaths and still my only thought was, *"Holy shit,"* as if my thinking mind had stuttered to a full stop.

In that moment, I could feel what that gap could cost me, the deep unworthiness that falseness always brings. Remember yoga means union, wholeness, and authenticity. It's remembering who we are and liking ourselves.

I had to give up the superb, Ivy-league-encrusted mask that she had offered to me. I just needed to be me. *"I am good enough to be interviewed on CNN. I am okay, even if I am not who they thought. What if they don't want me without the Princeton thing? I am enough, damn it. I am a yogi."* Mustering up the courage to say, *"I am not that,"* was hard, but being a pretender on international television would have been even harder. I watched the mask fall away, like the seductive, ephemeral, protection that it was. I reentered the ground of simple being.

> *Pretending to be something that I am not*
> *is based in the idea that I am not enough as I am.*

Pretending to be something that I am not is based in the idea that I am not enough as I am. That's where pretense comes from—it's the pretend version of you. I may not have attended Princeton, but I know some things about healing trauma with meditation and yogic philosophy. If I hide behind the pretty, glittery mask of pretense, I armor up. Yoga is the practice of disarming ourselves so we don't have to drag the weight of pretentiousness around.

I laughed—well, okay… I stammered, coughed, cleared my throat, then covered it all with a soft laugh. I smiled into that intimidating camera and said, "Oh, that was a colleague of mine, I did not lead that particular study, but here's what you need to know about healing trauma with yoga and meditation…" I exuded authority and confidence, because what else was I going to throw into that yawning gap? I am a people person, so I did what I do best. I leaned forward and connected with the reporter.

She was wonderful, a consummate pro and a delightful interviewer. She skillfully navigated our way forward together and even made it enjoyable. As I demonstrated anti-anxiety breathing, I faced the very real presence of my own stress. I used the exercise to release my tension, to be in the moment and practice what I preach. The news crew left happy, but as I closed the glass doors of our studio behind them, I spun around, leaned back, and bit my lips, a silent tear spilling down one cheek. *"Holy shit,"* I thought again, as I took a few more anti-anxiety breaths.

I felt that I was somehow tested that day. Am I living the teachings or am I using them to reinforce my ego? If I choose the latter, my sense of separation grows and the division between me and my realness increases. I move into the gap of separation and duplicity.

Yoga means union—becoming whole by skillfully traversing those tricky gaps. If I cannot love myself as I am, I am not practicing yoga.

I still get a little queasy at the memory of that moment, but it taught me about *satya*, the yogic teachings on truth. It revealed the indisputable value of befriending myself exactly as

I am, with all my unworthy, camera-shy complexities. I became my own ally that day. I stood beside myself, with myself, as myself. I stood up for being me as the pretense of desire and shame fell, like ash, like dust to the ground beneath me.

## Satya: My Truth Is Bigger Than Your Truth

We create chaos when we tell a lie, and that deception entangles us. All the threads of falseness are tied back to us, for we are their origin, their weaver, their first emergence. When we lie, we can't escape all that complication except through the truth. So, why lie? Why make life more complex? What are we dodging in the first place?

The yamas and niyamas—the principles framing this book—are sometimes called the don'ts and dos of yoga. The second of the five yamas, or the "don'ts," is *satya* in Sanskrit, meaning truth.

We lie because there's something about the truth that we believe can hurt, belittle, shame, expose, or somehow harm us or others. This belief creates the gap of duality. This is the space between reality and what we want to be true. The teachings of satya bridge this gap by guiding us back to an uncomplicated truth without pretense.

## Mind the Gap

There's a quality to the human mind that loves to divide and categorize. We attempt to solidify our own identity by reinforcing our opinions and ideas of what is outside us. We experience the world dualistically: "I am here. You are there.

We are apart." This judgmental quality lures us into "this is good, that is bad" thinking. It may extend back to primitive survival, to our ancestors foraging in the woods, exclaiming, "This mushroom is good, this mushroom can kill you." But this mental process creates separation. It creates "othering," or a culture of "us and them." By creating two camps, we generate division and blow apart cohesion. Anytime we experience a gap between ourselves and reality—like I did when the reporter presented a false version of me—two distinct paths open before us. If yoga is union, these multidimensional teachings will help us "mind the gap" and choose to be aligned with ourselves and our true purpose. We connect with reality instead of fighting against it, but we don't always live this way.

## But the Pizza Is Free

For example, we frequently commit to cleaning up our diet, drinking daily green smoothies, or forgoing sugar altogether. With great zeal and passion, we join the gym, secure a new workout partner, or hire a personal trainer. By lunchtime, however, when the office orders pizza and the spicy aroma of a handmade pie wafts in, we cave. Pizza is delicious. It's easier to imbibe in a fresh, hot slice than to stick with a new discipline, and hey, the pizza is free. This is duality. One part of us is pursuing growth and healthy new habits. Another equally strong part just wants the pizza. Duality has us yearning for two opposing experiences at the same time. This creates a powerful push and pull, an inner rift, a struggle of truly wanting to do one thing and yet choosing another. This is the gap of duality, and this is the gap that satya, truth, can heal.

Many people begin the satya practices with the idea that they don't lie, but as soon as they start to dig into these teachings, they see untruths they tell themselves every day. Like the daily lie of unloveability. There is no truth to that; no matter who you are, what you have done or what you have lived through, you are lovable. Love is your birthright. It's part of your inherent make-up. It's an undeniable aspect of who you are.

The Sanskrit word *sat* means "true essence" or "true nature" and "unchangeable." Yogis believe that in the deepest quiet of our true self is an already illumined being. At our very core, we are wide awake, conscious, and aware of our own sacred nature. Some might call this the soul, some might call it the light of consciousness, but this true, shining essence is the satya—the unshakable truth of pure being.

*Yogis believe that in the deepest quiet of our true self is an already illumined being. At our very core, we are wide awake, conscious and aware of our own sacred nature.*

## Getting Comfortable with Uncomfortable Truths

Studied in its deeper dimensions, satya is not just truth-telling, it is finding our authentic truth. It teaches us to see the radiant essence of ourselves underneath any adaptive behaviors.

The truth is not always easy. If we are going to get real with ourselves, honesty will often require us to leave our comfort zone and get comfortable with discomfort. Our growth zone is not typically inside our comfort zone. We grow when we stretch.

For example, let's say you were in an argument with a close friend and said something mean-spirited. In the heat of the moment, you crossed a line, and upon later reflection, you realize it. Satya asks you to open, get honest, and learn rather than close, deny, or defend. We have to be willing to look at our desire to be right or to look good—anything that's false or keeping our true self hidden behind the armor of pretense. The vulnerability of living truthfully and being our truest self does not ask us to go into the world unprotected. It asks us to go into the world undefended, un-false. Falseness, once exposed, begins to perish, and in this exposure process, we are liberated.

So, we develop the skill of being comfortable with uncomfortable truths. Admitting missteps. Exposing our imperfections. Learning. Apologizing well. We embrace the difficulty of clearing away what is not true to evolve into the truer self.

## MINI PRACTICE

### A MOMENT OF TRUTH

This mindfulness practice can give you access to your own true experience in any moment. Use it to allow yourself to simply feel what you feel.

#### Technique
Choose a word that feels true about you today, such as grateful, sad, hopeful, excited, anxious, strong, peaceful, or focused. Choose any word, any attribute. It can be positive or negative. The only prerequisite is that,

in the moment, it feels true. You may find it helpful to go with the idea that presents itself first rather than overthink it.

- Sit in a comfortable position and close your eyes.
- Use the attribute you would like to work with, for example, "anxious."
- Inhale, silently repeating your chosen attribute, "Breathing in anxiety, breathing out anxiety" or "Breathing in gratitude, breathing out gratitude." Insert your personal word of the day without judging yourself for how you actually feel. Use the word that best describes your current mood. Repeat this for three or more deep breaths.
- Then ask yourself, "Does it feel true?" Listen for the answer.
- Then ask, "Is there a deeper truth? What lies under this feeling?"
- If a deeper truth presents itself, do three breaths with that. For example, you could think, "Inhaling hurt, exhaling hurt," or "Inhaling calm, exhaling calm." Stay with it and allow it to take up space. You are not trying to change what you truly feel. You are attempting to identify and bear witness to it.
- If a deeper truth or experience does not present itself, no problem. Conclude where you are by opening and accepting that this is your truth in this moment.
- Be just as you are, accepting and not judging, even if you are feeling judgmental—just don't judge your process. Create a safe space for you to be truly as you are.

## Lost and Found in Texarkana

I was lost, alone, and driving my mom's dinged-up maroon Chevy through the middle of nowhere. I was adrift somewhere along the desolate Arkansas and Texas border, and I was seriously off course. The old, oversized paper map was spread out across the tan velour seat next to me, its creased graphics offering me little guidance. I decided to pull off the interstate, get gas, and ask for directions. I mean, how hard could it be to find the Texarkana Federal Penitentiary?

I was nineteen years old and traveling to visit my oldest brother. As I was flailing to finish my first year of college, uncertain of my life's direction, my parents made the dubious decision that I was the best candidate to visit my newly incarcerated sibling. He was ten years older than me and a full member of a notorious motorcycle gang. His Native American girlfriend and I had driven over six hundred miles together, but I deposited her in Little Rock, Arkansas, at her family reunion. In a ramshackle trailer park, I could almost feel the historic displacement and genocide of America's indigenous people. The place itself was heartbreaking, a cheap substitute for the bountiful lands these people once inhabited. Having spent the previous night wedged in among her threadbare extended family, crumpled into the top bunk of a disheveled mobile home, I felt hot, dirty, and anxious, trepidatious about entering a prison for the first time. The prison was just a couple hours away, and I would return to the tribe later that night.

My brother was there having been convicted of various crimes. My family constantly denied and purposely confused these accusations. It was an expert family trait, this sleight of hand, the smoke and mirrors of such thick denial that it was—and still is—impossible to perceive his crimes clearly. He was the eldest, born to the family pedestal, vehement in kicking it out from under his own feet, all the while clinging to its perks, privilege, and entitlement. Among the ambiguous legal charges were drug dealing, arson, battery, and human trafficking. My brother was accused—possibly convicted—of smuggling young Mexican women across the border to sell into prostitution.

With the hand-crank windows rolled down, hot air buffeting through the car, I took the next exit, which cloverleafed me directly into a redbrick Southern town square. I was cascaded into an inexplicable Saturday morning traffic jam with no available side streets, no outlet, and nowhere to pull off or turn around. I could see a scatter of parked black-and-white police cars ahead, lights flashing. Naively, I thought maybe this was the prison. But why would it be here, miles from my supposed destination? And why would it be in a small town's center? My car crawled to a stop and was slowly surrounded by a surge of aggressive men in white robes with ghostly hoods, streaming toward the square.

I was shocked. I couldn't believe it. I had inadvertently merged into a ragtag, seemingly disorganized Ku Klux Klan gathering.

I promptly started losing it. Shaking, I grasped the crumbly steering wheel with sweat-slick hands. Sitting, tall and alert, my eyes bugged wide and my heart rate accelerated. As my car inched forward, a young white cop with teardrop-shaped, mirrored sunglasses and a stubby dark blond mustache bent sideways to face me through the passenger side of my now tightly rolled up windows. He was smacking bright pink bubble gum, attitude and jaw muscles flexing hard. I could feel his stress clogging the space between us and I like to think he could feel mine. A side street was clearly visible behind him, blocked by old-fashioned sawhorse barricades. I pointed to my chest, then to the road at his back, indicating that I needed to go there. I desperately wanted to be anywhere but here. He glanced slowly left, then right. He shifted his hands on his thick black gun belt. He snapped his gum a few more times. Balancing the heavy barricade on one beefy hand, he gradually stepped backward.

He waved my car through.

All that happened in the briefest, most surreal moment. As I slid past the policeman, the change was shockingly abrupt, the unexpected storm of chaos and fear receding into a veneer of peace. Suddenly, I was cruising down a leafy, calm street in a lovely but simple small town. I drove for twenty minutes without stopping, without thinking, without vomiting, just putting distance between me and the visual violence I had witnessed. Blatant racism was being displayed boldly, in broad daylight. Set on seeing my brother, I drove on.

After signing into the prison, I walked into the holding area. I was midway between being fully in the prison and fully in the free world. I felt the cold rush of air vacuuming past my body as the hard metal door sealed into place behind me. I faced the short, uniformed female guard as she explained that she would need to search me bodily. I stood, spread-eagle, facing the male guard as she started patting me down. She brushed her hand across my crotch. Twice. Three times. Squeezing. The male guard grinned, his lascivious gaze slow and penetrating, looking me down and up, down, and up. In unison, they choreographed a hidden dance of invasive sleaze.

The door popped open, and I grabbed my gifts for my brother. Reese's Pieces were a hot new fad and I had brought a few bags for him, all now missing. Blowing out my breath, I entered a dingy cafeteria-style room with families visiting, cheap molded plastic chairs screeching across scarred lino-leum floors.

I sat at an empty, circular table to await his arrival, attempting to feel and not feel the barrage of this day. As he neared, I stood, and we hugged. I can't really imagine what being in prison is like, and I'm pretty sure that day I became the most law-abiding citizen I possibly could. I never, ever wanted to live in his choices, to stand in his government-is-sued shoes. The environment felt so purposefully out of con-trol and dehumanizing. The power of choice seemed to have been taken—or given—away. I was unnerved, repulsed by all of it; the specter of the Klansmen was still flitting at the edge of my mind, as well as the guard's abusive touch.

I caught my brother up on all the family shenanigans. I shared the books they had carefully curated for his stay. Some random candy—smooth tubes of Lifesavers, a sticky red Tootsie Roll Pop—kept rolling around in the bottom of the box with a couple soft, white T-shirts, socks, and under-wear. He told me he would try to work in the kitchen, because, you know, food—the glue of our family. I was scheduled to return with his girlfriend the next day for one more visit, then she and I would drive away. A few minutes before our allotted visiting time was up, he leaned forward—but not too far forward—in his chair. The guards would call you out if you got too close after that initial, fully observed hug.

"Can you sneak me in some drugs tomorrow?"

## A Coalescence of Worth

My family was sexist, probably born of a ravenous Irish his-tory of needing the boys and the men to keep the family alive. The throwaway people were the girls. When my brother made his astonishing request, the thought never occurred to him to be concerned that, if caught, I too would be imprisoned. He had also never thought about whether or not to use another of our siblings as cover in a gang shootout. He had held my sister's body in front of his while bullets went flying, so if anyone got shot it would be her, not him. In his eyes, she was a throwaway person. In his eyes, so was I.

Listening to his request, I stammered. I should have blasted him for the blatant lack of true brothering, but this is the culture I was raised in. This is what I would need to transcend. Take care of the boys at all costs, even if they are behaving with astounding selfishness. The girls are dispensable.

That night, horrifyingly, I pondered ways to sneak drugs into a federal prison. I wanted to bypass that creepy, gropy guard, maybe just to get one over on her. I knew I would never do it, but this day pounded against me, prying me open, breaking me down. I was mired in a familial realm of misery and suffering, all of us held captive by the oppressive sludge of toxic self-loathing. I had to free myself of this but had no idea how.

On the two-hour drive back to Little Rock, I thought about what I would risk by carrying drugs into a federal penitentiary. All that night I lay in the trailer's musty top bunk, silently arguing with my brother, kicking against the thin coverlet, voiceless in the dark. I was wrestling with a truth that was shattering my rose-colored image of my convict brother. How that image had lasted so long is beyond me.

The next morning, over lukewarm corn-mush cereal with dark-eyed children all around me, I felt a thickening of inner resolve, a coalescence of worth. I did not smuggle drugs into a Texas prison. I looked into his belligerent, drug-lusting eyes and told him I did not have anything to give him. His scorn was palpable. As I faced down his sneering disappointment, I chose me.

The brutality of that day both destroyed and created something, which echoes one of the ideas behind real yoga: you have to destroy your unworthiness to give birth to your worth.

*You have to destroy your unworthiness*
*to give birth to your worth.*

I was in the present moment, and I was changing. This insight made the lengthy drive home from Texas even more potent than the experiences I had on that trip because I let myself change. I let myself process. I let myself feel and accept—or at least briefly touch—the blind-hot rage at being maneuvered, manhandled, and tossed to the side. I let myself release some things instead of burying them in the graveyard of my being.

I entered that prison voiceless, but my shackled silence was coming loose. As my brother's girlfriend and I sped home, she was exhausted and spent, so she kept sleeping. I kept driving, fueled by frosty Coca-Cola and loud eighties music blaring from the staticky radio—Pat Benatar belting "Hit Me with Your Best Shot." Fat hot tears came. Some dark internal behemoth began a slow subterranean shift, an ancient soul awareness ascending, breaking free. I had chosen me. I could do it again.

## The Crucible of Becoming

I was finding my way into making a different choice, into choosing my way out of the family darkness. I had acted and changed myself in a way that I couldn't fully identify, obscured by the family pattern—the belief that I was not good enough. I decided I would never make the self-destructive choices that would land me in prison. A path that would give voice to throwaway people had to exist. It had to.

*The toolkit of yoga guides you through a process of yoking all your broken fragments back together into the true, whole version of you.*

The toolkit of yoga guides you through a process of yoking all your broken fragments back together into the true, whole version of you. If this truth really exists in me—as my dog-eared copy of the *Bhagavad Gita* claims—I wasn't a lesser person, no matter what my family believed. I had more work to do to strengthen my spindly teenage backbone, to crawl up out of the ancestral sludge, and to find a clear voice and sing, shout, and bellow my way into wholeness.

It is this truth, this irrefutable value that we all embody—all of us. The trip to Texarkana was the birthplace of my social justice activism, but I didn't fully comprehend it at the time. I felt an essential innermost truth stirring within me. I just did not yet know how to claim it.

I had no role models for embodied truth, but I did have an extravagance of examples for what not to do, how not to live. I was refusing the alcoholism, the brokenness, and the self-loathing. I was standing at a significant junction in my life—a soul pivot, a true turning point. I was yearning for something more genuine and satisfying. I chose the teachings of satya, to help me find my true voice and ultimately show me my way home.

# The Truth of Social Justice

Mahatma Gandhi used the term *satyagraha*, the truth that grabs hold of you and will not let go. He used this yoga-based concept in his civil rights efforts to free India from British enslavement. He demanded equality between English and Indian citizens, claiming this simple truth: the English are not superior to the Indians they colonized.

Gandhi has been criticized for not taking satya far enough because he was not willing to take on India's caste system or unconcealed sexism or ageism. But Gandhi's groundbreaking equality work provided a model for American civil rights activist Dr. Martin Luther King, Jr., and many others. King studied and applied Gandhi's system of nonviolent social change to guide him. Both Gandhi and Dr. King translated satyagraha as soul force—the opposite of brute force—using yoga's ethics and ideals to instigate social change. Using yogic wisdom teachings to catalyze personal and social change is how you can use yoga's spiritual principles across cultures without misappropriating them.

So, if you are a marginalized person—through race, gender identity, sexual orientation, age, physical ability, language, or immigration status—you have the heightened challenge of learning how to love yourself in a society that does not clearly reflect your value back to you. In a recent conversation with Peloton yoga star Dr. Chelsea Jackson Roberts, who is a longtime student of mine, she shared, "My yoga practice is pointless if it doesn't support justice."

Gandhi and King gave us a template to use these ancient teachings to fight for all people to be seen as valuable, which is the irrevocable truth of humanity. Many yogis are using the yamas and niyamas as tools of equality to create more equity in the world. We can do this by supporting present-day civil rights issues, like the work currently being done to ensure the safety of trans youth in schools. We could support the overdue, necessary effort to safeguard Black lives and Black votes. We can use these teachings to become more aware and put that awareness into action. Satya holds the truth that in our diversity and interconnectedness, we all belong to the sacred. We do not have to earn love—we are love. None of us are free until all of us are free, and that is the truth that sets everyone free.

## DEEP PRACTICE

### INFINITY BREATH

Many people seem to barely breathe. They stress breathe: short and shallow, high and tight, focused up in their chest and shoulders. Yogis, however, are known for deep, languorous breathing: vast belly breaths that visibly move the diaphragm and lungs. These breaths take up space. They make noise. They connect you to your sense of being fully in the moment. These breaths remind you of your deepest inner truth.

Yogic breathing practices contain real magic because if you can change your breath, you can change your mind. Albert Einstein said, "No problem can be solved on the same level of consciousness that created it." In yoga, we advise students, when your mind is stuck, ignore it and go to the breath. There is infinite possibility in a well-taken breath. It is that infinity we connect to through this practice.

*If you can change your breath,*
*you can change your mind.*

The Infinity Breath can create a vast sense of spaciousness where we can relax into being more genuine. By lengthening your respiratory pattern, this powerhouse practice slows your heart rate, which in turn calms your nervous system. It is an excellent method to help reduce tension and anxiety, so you can get a glimpse of the deeper truth within yourself.

**Infinity Mudra:** This practice utilizes a *mudra*, a sacred hand gesture, to direct attention and energy. Touch the fingertips of both hands together. Each finger of your left hand will lightly touch the corresponding finger of your right hand. Create a sphere-like space between your hands, as if you were lightly holding a globe between them. Place the mudra comfortably in front of your belly, chest, or even in your lap. Sustain a light pressure between the fingertips.

**Ujjayi Breath:** This practice utilizes yoga's classic Ujjayi breath sound, which you learned in Chapter One's Mini Practice. To employ Ujjayi, make a soft "hhhhh" sound as you breathe through your nose, like a sighing sound at the base of your throat.

*Technique*
- Sit for meditation with your hands in the Infinity Mudra.

- Set an intention to experience roominess within yourself.
- Inhale a slow, deep Ujjayi breath through your nose.
- Puckering your lips as if you are blowing out a candle, exhale through your mouth, gently blowing.
- Retain the pucker and inhale through your mouth, almost like drawing air in through a straw.
- Exhale with Ujjayi sound through your nose. That is one round of Infinity Breath.
- Continue to alternate: inhale nose, exhale mouth, then inhale mouth, exhale nose.
- As you inhale, give yourself space. As you exhale, give yourself time.
- Continue the Infinity Breath for eleven minutes, using long, deep breaths.
- Create spaciousness with your breath until you feel spacious. Feel consciousness expanding within you, connecting you to your true self.

**A Word to the Wise:** Sometimes when you embark on a new *pranayama*, or yogic breath practice, it can make you lightheaded or dizzy. This sensation is your own body cautioning you to pause and take a few normal breaths until the dizziness passes. You are expanding your *prana*—your life force—and it takes some adjustment to hold more of this lifeforce energy. You are energetically adjusting to accommodate your own growth and to sustain growth at a manageable rate.

.

# 3
# STEALING
# SELF-WORTH

**Asteya:** (uhh-STAY-uh) non-stealing

*"There is nothing enlightened about shrinking so other
people won't feel inadequate around you. We are all
meant to shine..."*

MARIANNE WILLIAMSON

## Stop Stealing the Shirt Off My Back

I stormed downstairs, incredulous, in the small riverfront
hotel—a guest house, really—situated on the banks of the
Ganges River in the ancient city of Varanasi. This was the final
stop on a monthlong sojourn through India. This pilgrimage
place bore the original name of Kashi, the holy city of Shiva,
the city of light, the revered abode of the yogis. Experiencing this sacred site was a lifelong dream for me, but over the
course of a month, India had worn me down, peeled me open,
stood me on my head and laid me bare, as only India can do.

I did yoga with chickens rollicking in and out of a feath-
er-strewn practice room.

I shivered under damp, skeevy blankets.

I respectfully witnessed sacred funeral pyres burn, bodies and bones crumbling slowly to ash.

I clambered over riverside boulders, placing my hand upon human skull after human skull, then plunged into the depths of that icy Himalayan river.

I ate some of the best food of my life.

I bowed as holy men anointed my forehead with vibrant red *tilak*.

I rubbed shoulders with sleepy elephants.

I escaped from crazy, screaming monkeys.

I was swept up in a *sadhu* parade, merging with a torrent of holy people, chanting and dancing down the middle of a random, winding neighborhood street.

But dammit, someone had stolen my clothes again—for the umpteenth time on this trip—and I just couldn't take it.

The third restraint of the *Yoga Sutra* is *asteya,* or not stealing. Coveting, stealing, and taking what is not ours is based on the idea that we are not whole, that we need something outside ourselves to be okay. Asteya says: don't lift the packet of mints, don't leave the gathering with someone else's scarf, don't charge personal items on your boss's card, and don't take credit for someone else's work. It means do not steal. And do not swipe someone else's outfits from their locked Indian hotel rooms.

I learned this yogic principle in the US, but here I was in India, the land of yoga's holy teachings, getting my belongings stolen in every single place I visited. The irony is laughable, but the deeper intention of asteya is to address scarcity thinking. As an American traveling in India, I had more food, more clothes, more privilege, more... material possessions than most people on that continent ever would.

However, my entitled, shabbily dressed self was on a roll of self-righteousness, so I marched my angry, huffing form right up to the affable concierge and poured out my story of woe. With a perfect hallmark Indian head waggle, he smiled and said, "That is not possible."

Astonished at the ludicrous denial, but also the absurdity of the situation, I stopped, speechless. I was worn down. I was not ready to fully relinquish my ire, but I stood no chance against the tide of something utterly out of my control. I lowered my head to the desk and slumped forward, exasperated.

I paused.

Inhaling, I rose up, pointer finger raised, to jump back into the fray, looked him in the eye, and saw the sparkle of humor there. It dislodged a tiny bit of something in me; my breath blew out, and my perspective shifted very slightly to one side.

I stood incredulous in the lobby, suddenly aware of my lifelong struggle with not-enoughness. I, who had so much, so ridiculously much, was standing in a country that had given me life-changing tools of wisdom while her citizens had so few worldly goods. It felt like my mind was bending and contorting around itself. I was trying to not be the victim of thievery, to remain indignant, as well as to defend my not-enoughness stance. I was discovering that in the deeper reality of that moment… I was okay. I was disgruntled, sure, but the people stealing from me were probably truly affected by need. I, in contrast, as a middle-income American, was not really that needy—but my mind still was.

For me, this is what a moment of ego death is like. Feeling a part of my belief system—my demanding, not-enoughness mind—withering and dying while I am simultaneously trying to keep it alive. I touched into my own argument with reality, my desire for something to be different than it was. I was sick of people stealing my clothes. But if I could muster up understanding or resignation, acceptance, or compassion, even a sense of humor, could I learn something here? What was India trying to teach me?

## Asteya: Stealing Self-Worth

In the Four Noble Truths, the Buddha taught that "desire is the root of all suffering." Let's face it—we are a consumer culture. We want things: people, jobs, relationships, houses, cars, shoes. Nothing is wrong with the desire to have a good life and live abundantly. Feeling like we have enough to be okay is satisfying, and so is enjoying the nice, pricey stuff.

The deeper teachings of yoga's third restraint, *asteya*, offer insight into scarcity thinking, which is the chronic behind-the-scenes belief that gives us sticky fingers in the first place. Not-enoughness occurs when need becomes insatiable, and more always leads to wanting more. We somehow believe that an acquisition—a title, a relationship, a cupcake, a raise, or a certain number of followers—will fill our internal desire and make us feel like we are enough. Here, we touch into our own inner hunger, our elemental need.

We all have normal human needs: to be loved, safe, and connected, to be relevant, to belong. In a scarcity-based belief system, however, we think our solutions are outside us, that our hidden, emotional hungers could somehow be filled by external means. This is a mistake of the intellect. We are incredible, complex social creatures. Yet sometimes we feel disconnected and alone.

Inner hunger is a hunger for spirit. It is a hunger to know love from the inside out, to be loved, to feel loved, to identify our connection to our sacred source, and to merge into the actuality of love. Once we realize both the problem and the solution are within, we realize what we seek cannot be stolen from within or without. Our essential okayness—our sacred aliveness—can only be uncovered, realized, and remembered.

> *"To heal inner hunger is to claim*
> *belonging as your birthright.*
> *To embody self-worth."*

To heal inner hunger is to claim belonging as your birthright. It means to embody self-worth. Standing in that hotel lobby, feeling my belief system disintegrate and reform within me, I discovered an aspect of my mind that was more generous, more aligned, and more immersed in love. I relaxed into the unrelenting chaos that is India—that really, is the world. I saw the duality, the deep divide of not-enoughness thinking, and the union of yoga drawing me back into oneness. I realized it was okay. I was okay. Well, that and maybe I needed some more clothes.

## Godiva Is the Devil

I was a relatively new swami—an ordained teacher and leader—in an unorthodox, full-throttle, yoga *shakti* lineage, and I was hungry, stressed, and a little cranky. In a shakti tradition, there is an emphasis on awakening *kundalini*, the raw energy of transformation that lies curled at the base of the spine. Kundalini transforms into shakti when it passes through our inner heart and is infused with love. Once awakened, shakti makes us feel deeply alive, sometimes even lit up, but it can also light up and illuminate anything we feel. So, if we feel angry, abandoned, or deeply deprived, we experience an intensified, fully embodied version of our original feeling. It's like turning up the dial on the emotional body with the intention of "feel it to heal it." Shakti strips away the surface coping mechanisms for deep emotion, leaving us a little wilder and more unedited than we are in our everyday modality.

Needless to say, some emotional maturity is needed to handle this, and when we feel stretched thin, our emotional maturity thins out as well. All of us are in a perpetual process of growing and healing our wounds—including illuminated teachers, yogis and spiritual seekers. That includes baristas, CEOs, artists, and social justice advocates. That includes yoga teachers, yoga students, and scorners of all things yoga. None of us is fully evolved, so sometimes in the provocative process of our unfolding, moments of being really human happen. We make mistakes. We act from ego. We feel our selfish desires and relentless hungers surge to the surface of our consciousness with reckless abandon. In other words, we can become irrationally angry, tearful, or ravenous.

So here I was at my guru's ashram, in the lush summer heat, rushing and muggy with perspiration from the midday Florida sun. I was dressed in marigold and fuchsia, ready to attend a *darshan* or spiritual discourse with my esteemed teacher. My comfy cotton outfit was sticking to my sweat-slicked back, and as I entered her deep-freeze air-conditioned rooms, I paused, puffing my top in and out, feeling the cool air touch my skin. We were midway through a weekend intensive with students from all over the world, many of them from my urban yoga ashram in Atlanta.

The effect of the weekend's offerings was stirring up my own stuff, and I was straddling the roles of being both student and teacher. I was tardy, unfed, hot, and a bit flustered, having spent the entire lunch hour consoling one of my students about her dissolving marriage. She was justifiably brokenhearted, and I found myself juggling her emotions and my own stress about showing up late to escort my guru into an event that would last, uninterrupted, until dinner. My physical hunger was real but something about that day was touching a deeper, inner hunger as well. I felt a raw kind of want at the back of my throat as I dashed into the building. The thick black carpet felt good against my bare feet as I wove my way back though Ma's private quarters to the intimacy of her tiny in-house hair salon, where one of her students was arranging her long, black hair.

The room was tight with devotees, most of them swamis. The eldest two, one from New York, the other from LA, were in among the others. They were both gay men who adored Ma but could pierce you with a well-aimed barb, like the snarkiest of queens. The room was crammed with an ongoing influx of gifts, presents, and flower arrangements for Ma's birthday celebration. Ma's students relished showering her with extravagant expressions of love, from stupendous cakes shaped like her beloved Coney Island to gorgeous sparkly workout clothes, bejeweled in the latest fashion. Being around Ma was really fun in these moments. Watching her joy was delightful, even infectious.

One of my students who was unable to attend the event sent in a tower of Godiva chocolate—literally. A five-foot-tall stack of luxe boxes overflowed with hundreds of rich gooey caramels, creamy dark truffles, and startlingly sweet confections. Ma gleefully pried open the first box and bit into a morsel, whimpering with gastronomic delight. She kept opening bigger and bigger packages, trying one from each in a jubilant cacophony of candy. As she passed around the containers, the elder swami sitting next to me kept passing them over my head. Now—full disclosure—chocolate is my thing. I am a self-avowed dark chocolate aficionado, and I watched in silent wonder as everyone in the room except for me descended on the open treasure.

At first, I thought, *Well, okay, whatever. Godiva isn't my favorite chocolate anyway.* But the feeling of being left out materialized. I felt uncertainty—was he intentionally passing me over? Was he poking at something in me? The feeling of exclusion started to stir something painful within, constricting the back of my throat. I watched as my irritation grew, tasting the hot slick of shame, of somehow not being good enough. Remember that shakti, or spiritual energy, is designed to peel away your coping mechanisms and pull back the mask to reveal what is not yet healed.

I felt the all-too-familiar pang of elemental hunger from deep within the heart of my upbringing. My family was a pack of foodies, all of us a little bit addicted to food and a little bit hungry for something perpetually out of reach. I breathed. I listened to that aching, gnawing force. I recognized my not-enoughness, fueled by the competition of six older siblings, shoving their love-starved selves to the forefront. I knew the Godiva chocolates were not the issue, nor was the non-inclusive behavior. But as the box, brimming over with chocolates, was passed over my head once again, I reached up and snagged a truffle, breathing in its spicy warm scent. I touched the smooth outer shell to my lips, broke it open with my teeth, and sucked in the velvet interior.

Suddenly, we all rose to escort Ma out to begin her discourse, opened boxes strewn haphazardly across the floor.

Seated in the back, I politely waited to exit last. Just as the final person vanished from my view, I reached down into a box of truffles. I lifted and devoured one after another, two, then three, then four, eating the unoffered love, consuming the flavor of unfillable longing.

My heart pounding with sugar, deviousness, and a disorienting satisfaction, I walked into the guru's living room, where the other swamis were milling around, awaiting Ma, who was touching up her lipstick. Everyone had a sugar buzz, now, including me. Standing enormous on one side of the room, a life-sized statue of the Black goddess Kali wielded a blood-soaked sword. Her weapon is symbolic of slaying the insatiable mind—exactly what I was encountering within myself that day. Kali is wild, determined, and outrageous. She is the goddess who takes suffering, who reveals illusion, and who frees us from our bondage to self-limiting habits.

"Take this from me, Kali," I whispered as we processed out the doors and into the meditation hall. I was offering up my hunger, my chocolate addiction, my yearning, and my strife.

## *"It only comes up to be healed..."*

"It only comes up to be healed" is a mantra of compassion I share with my students often, especially when their issues are stirred up. Our suffering arises from within us so we can heal it. It does not resurface to torture us again or for us to repeat patterns or marinate in the pain. It comes up because a lesson has yet to be learned, a wound has not quite healed. I was attempting to offer empathy to myself, to live what I teach. I made the offering, released the need, and opened myself to the teachings of the day.

# MINI PRACTICE

## I AM FULL, I AM LOVED

This is an affirmation-based practice to reveal neediness and address unresolved inner hunger. It is simple and effective. It is designed to expose, then relinquish, longing and unworthiness. It creates purposeful satiation and fulfillment, which ultimately reconnect you to simply being and being okay as you are.

### Technique

You can do this practice anytime, anywhere. You can repeat the phrase silently to yourself or out loud as a continuous mantra.

Simply say, "I am filled by my beloved. I am full. I am loved." Repeat until you feel full and loved. Use this practice to create and experience a sense of personal satiation.

## Lions and Tigers and Monks, Oh My

While public speaking stretches me more than any yoga pose ever could, sharing the wisdom of yoga with marginalized folks lights me up. I love it. So, as a novice teacher, I continued to lead contemplative arts for AIDS and HIV+ classes at Grady, Atlanta's inner-city hospital. The more I taught, the more the mystical teachings—tantra, kundalini, hatha and vinyasa—entwined themselves in me. My teaching style was creating and defining itself.

However, I still felt staunchly unworthy about teaching. I had accrued yoga teacher training certificates in a multitude of styles and was qualified at the highest level in the US accreditation system. I was an avid learner but had refused many teaching gigs because getting up and being the one who knows made me nervous. Really nervous.

The weekly Grady class had just been relocated to the Infectious Diseases Clinic. The space was new, clean, even pristine—a massive upgrade from the dank, depressing hospital basement where our class was previously held. One summer evening, as I unrolled my yoga mat at the front of the sunny classroom, one of the regulars approached. A lissome gay man in his midthirties, Trent leaned in and whispered to me that the nurses assigned to the HIV+ ward were all talking about my classes. A few had slipped into the last few sessions and said they were finding real relief from the onslaught of burnout. Currently, a tight, inquisitive pack of nurses was peeking around the entryway to the room, asking if they could attend and surreptitiously pulling several doctors in with them.

Of course, I welcomed them with open arms. All of us need to drink as we pour, especially those on the frontlines of the helping professions. But internally, I was freaking out. I couldn't teach doctors! I'm just a meditating, blissed-out yoga girl. Having already experienced an inner meltdown when the nurses started showing up, what was I supposed to do with this? What if I said your liver is on the wrong side of the body? What if I said something to make the medical professionals scoff or roll their eyes? Here was my old friend—perennial unworthiness—showing up to accompany me as I taught. What if I don't know enough? What if I'm not good enough to teach doctors?

This belief in my not-enoughness lay at the core of my never-ending accumulation of accreditation. My belief was this: no matter how much I studied and learned, I didn't know enough. This translated to not being good enough. This was the relentless mantra of my upbringing: I am not enough. My family could step on me hundreds of times a day, belittling the confidence out of me, one sarcastic insult at a time. It was a scathing, soul-crushing miasma of learned, inherited unworthiness. The bubbling hope I took from practicing yoga and meditation was the best remedy I had found. So, I educated and immersed myself. I read book after book, absorbing as much as I could: underlining, extrapolating, discussing, sharing. I took course after course, exploring all of it: how to embody, how to articulate, how to demonstrate, and how to teach.

All of this accrued knowledge began to unravel with one friendly, Ivy League doctor walking into the room. He pulled off his badge, his white coat, and his aura of authority, plunked down, and joined the group. I took a deep breath and sat down as well, winding my legs into each other, tucking into the classic seat of a yogi. I sat tall, introduced the day's topic, and taught through my nerves and my unworthiness. My voice shook a little, warbling out the introductory mantra. My knees were jiggly as well, but no one could see their tremors in my cross-legged pose. I did my imperfect best, teaching, sharing, and seeking out the rhythm of deep practice that was always there, flowing beyond my fear-entangled mind. I tried to use my lack of self-worth as fuel. It was patchy, but basically, I didn't die—at least not right away.

### The Unstealable Thing

Here I was—so fearless, so brave—undone by a terrifying, kind, young doctor. I was shaking in my metaphoric shoes, since, of course, I was unshod. I attempted to establish a foundation of self-worth while facing down my legacy of shame. I felt complicated, convoluted, and confused in a space I normally felt fluid, affable, and free. Yoga, breath, and meditation were my safe spaces. Even though I often felt anxious teaching in front of a large or new group, I loved sharing, and sharing what you love is infectious.

*Healing the not-enoughness mind*
*is the real work of asteya, not stealing.*

Healing the not-enoughness mind is the real work of asteya, not stealing. Our self-worth belongs to us. It belongs inside us. It's the unstealable thing that gets obscured, distorted, given away, and stolen all the time. We don't want it stolen—from us, or by us—because our sense of self is the foundation for our happiness. Yet our fear of inadequacy is sneaky, undermining confidence at every turn. If we trust that we are okay when we win or lose, rise, or fall, we embody self-worth. Our sense of being enough and belonging then connects us to love. We remember that we are lovable, no matter what. Our ability to be confident enough to pour what we love into the world changes both us and the environment around us.

In her groundbreaking work, shame researcher Dr. Brené Brown explains the difference between guilt and shame. Guilt is what we feel when we have done something harmful and see our behavior as a problem. Shame is what we feel when we have done something harmful and see ourselves as the problem. Guilt says, "I did something bad." Shame says, "I *am* something bad." I had learned shame as a way of being in the world. I had been taught that I would never measure up, that I had no right to stand at the front of any room. Shame may have been put upon me, but it is my work to free myself from it.

## Killing Me Softly

The following week, my Grady class was packed. Word was out that we were having fun—in a hospital in the face of the AIDS epidemic—breathing deeply, finding our way back to center, and reconnecting to joy. After surviving my own self-created ordeal of teaching the doctor, I realized it was time for me to learn how to teach anyone, to not get caught in who I was teaching but to just show up and share, no matter who is in the room. This realization was a shame destroyer. Teaching wasn't about me; it was about what was being shared. I was just the vessel. I was learning as much as I was teaching. The doctor, a gay anesthesiologist in recovery from drug addiction, became a regular attendee of the class. As our friendship developed over the next few months, I learned about his struggles, his issues with self-worth, and his healing journey. Because all of us have one.

## The Last Laugh

The very next week, midtown traffic was thick, so I was rushing to class, a little bit late, squeezing time. I bounced into the room feeling pretty good, maybe even with a tinge of confidence. The doctor's mystique was demystified. My sense of self was back in its place, tenuously centered inside of me. Dropping my bag onto the floor, I kicked off my sandals, turned and glanced up, ready to connect and delve into practice together. Just then, a Tibetan Buddhist monk walked into class, maroon and saffron robes flowing, shaved head flashing in the glare of the overhead lights. I froze. He and I nodded and bowed awkwardly at each other, shyly looking eye to eye. We both calmly rolled out our yoga mats. I then excused myself to the bathroom and had a private, outraged little temper tantrum.

I only shouted in my mind.

"WTF? What kind of joke is God playing? I can't teach a monk! Stop testing me! This is as much vulnerability as I can handle!"

I shook it off. Strode back into the room. The monk and I sparkled at each other.

We were grinning, bowing, acknowledging, honoring. Did I detect a bit of bravado in him? Or was that me? Teaching the doctor had revealed an ability to open and connect when I wanted to contract and hide. I was learning to soften in my own unworthiness, to not take my negative thoughts so seriously.

Like the doctor, the monk and I got to know each other. Whenever he was in America, he would drop into class. One afternoon, after the session had ended, he and I were hanging out on the floor, feeling the yoga glow, the rich silence of the closing meditation suspended softly in the air between us. I told him I was intimidated to teach him. He told me, as a gay HIV+ monk, he had found a sense of acceptance in our group. Even he had felt shame, the great separator, the thief of belonging.

We stood up and hugged, then caught up with the other students and all went out for Thai food. And I wondered— looked forward to—who would show up to class the next week, to teach me to stretch a little bit more.

## The Too-Muchness of Not-Enoughness

Not-enoughness also has a companion belief: too-muchness. They are opposite sides of the same coin—twin facets of the same coping mechanism. We do too much, overachieving to address our lack of worth. We struggle to establish a sense of self by striving, stealing, acquiring, accomplishing, competing, or proving. The teachings of asteya ask us to center our worth within ourselves rather than trying to get worth from what we do in the world. This is tricky because we like to contribute and succeed. Our successes are wonderful, but we are worthwhile without them. If we fail, we are just as lovable as we were before our failure. We are just as worthy of kind regard—just as worthy of everything.

Too-muchness is a breeding ground for overwhelm and burnout. Ironically, when people say "it is all too much" they are operating in scarcity thinking, riding the pendulum from not enough to too much, flying past the middle ground of genuine self-worth. When we habitually overcommit and overextend, we are trying to prove we are good enough by our output. So how do we separate our worthiness from our accomplishments?

One method is to actively separate guilt and shame. When we fail at something, can we know that we tried our best, even if we made a bad decision? Can we fall short and be compassionate toward ourselves? We may feel bad that we failed or screwed something up, but can we make mistakes without creating shame? Can we kindly laugh at ourselves? Can we say "oops, really sorry" when we hurt others? Accountability radically facilitates this process of acknowledging the error, apologizing well, and standing in the apology undefended. When we do this, shame burns in the fire of authenticity. We allow ourselves the grace of imperfection and create space for our humanity and everyone else's.

*Shame burns in the fire of authenticity.*

## Wasting Time

Our relationship with time is also a powerful indicator of our "enoughness." Do you believe you have an abundance of time? Or do you rush around, overcommitted, late for everything? This distorted association with time has almost become the norm in modern culture. When we are habitually late, we steal time from other people while simultaneously stealing well-being from ourselves. We create unnecessary stress for everyone involved.

Procrastination generates another distorted dance with time and self-worth, robbing us of the simplicity of feeling good about ourselves. When we procrastinate, we take away our ability to be in the moment. We stop taking care of ourselves and our lives. We steal satisfaction from ourselves. This produces stress because we haven't gotten things done. It also reinforces unworthiness, the root belief that we ourselves are not enough.

*Not-enoughness and too-muchness are*

*the currency of the ego—the fear-based mind.*

Not-enoughness and too-muchness are the currency of the ego—the fear-based mind. They touch every facet of our lives: Do we give ourselves time? Do we give ourselves space to try things? To feel? To fail? Asteya heals the scarcity mind by giving us a tool to examine and change our relationship to the hungry mind.

# DEEP PRACTICE

## DRINKING THE MOON

The yogis of old would pay wise attention to their natural surroundings, attuning themselves to the rhythm of nature, the cadence of the planets, the tidal push-pull of the rivers and oceans. They honored the rising of the sun each day with a *vinyasa*, a flowing cycle of postures known as the Sun Salutation. They chanted each evening as the sun set over the horizon, thanking the radiant orb for its beauty and bounty, anticipating its return the next morning. Based on the lunar calendar, they developed rituals and ceremonies to honor the sun and the moon. These wisdom-keepers experienced the rhythms of nature reflected both in the sensory world around them and the world of spirit within them. They felt they were a vital part of the natural world, and that this world was alive inside them. The term *hatha yoga* translates as sun-moon union, indicating a balance of these natural energies: sun-moon, hot-cold, external-internal, radiant-reflective, yang-yin. These universal energies are what a yogi strives to keep in harmonious union.

An easy way to deepen your awareness of the planets is through increasing your attentiveness to the moon. The phases of the moon influence the waters of the earth, the pulse of the rivers and oceans, as well as the circadian rhythms of your body. By "drinking" the energy of the moon, you fill your cup. I do a monthly Vedic Full Moon ceremony to create a connection between me and the cycles of the moon and to honor the passage of time. Here is a simple vinyasa—a fluid series of movements to increase your connection to the moon.

### Moon Cooling Breath + Moon Mudra Vinyasa

This Kali Natha Yoga practice—the yoga of my root lineage, taught directly to me by my guru, Ma Jaya— pairs a breath, a mudra and a vinyasa. Mudra, in Sanskrit, means seal. The most widely known mudra is Prayer Pose, sealing our palms together in a gesture of humility. The mudras direct energy, and for this practice, we will be directing our focus to the cooling, calming energy of the moon.

**Half Moon Mudra:** Make a "C" shape with each hand. Wrap the right hand around the left to make a half moon shape.

**Sitali Breath:** *Sitali* means cooling, like the energy of the moon. Curl your tongue like a straw. Stick your tongue a little way out of the mouth. Inhale deeply through the curled tongue. Retract the tongue into the mouth, curl it up touching the tip of the tongue on the roof of the mouth, back where the hard and soft palette meet. Close your lips and exhale through the nose. Continue this practice with long, deep breaths. If you are unable to curl the tongue, simply inhale across the surface of the tongue.

**Half Moon Mudra Vinyasa:**
- Place the hands in Half Moon Mudra in front of your belly.
- Inhaling, release the hands as you sweep the arms out to the sides, then up overhead into the Half Moon Mudra, symbolizing the moon overhead.
- Exhaling, sweep the arms down and create the Half Moon Mudra behind your back near your sacrum.
- Inhaling, circle your hands out to the sides then straight out in front of your chest in Half Moon Mudra.
- Place your hands in Prayer Pose, then pull the Prayer Pose into your chest, honoring your heart.

**Putting It All Together: Drinking the Moon**
- Sit for meditation.
- Place your hands in Half Moon Mudra, resting comfortably against your body or in your lap.
- Take eleven or more Sitali breaths, breathing very deeply. As you do this, visualize the moon on your forehead at your third eye and ask for your mind to become calm and reflective. Imagine drinking in the cooling essence of the moon.
- After completing the breath, do the Moon Mudra Vinyasa three to twelve times.

This moon practice awakens the reflective qualities of your mind. It symbolically places you in the center of the cycles of the moon. It cools down internal hunger and gives you access to an innate sense of fullness and enoughness as you "drink in" the moon's abundant energy.

# 4
# WALKING WITH THE SACRED

**Brahmacharya:** (bruhm-HUH-char-yuh)
wise use of energy, sexual moderation

*"Knowing how to be solitary is central to the art of loving.*
*When we can be alone, we can be with others without*
*using them as a means of escape."*

BELL HOOKS

## But I Thought You Were Gay

"What are you doing here with your beautiful girlfriend anyway... I thought you were gay."

Ma's words to Jacques echoed across the pin-drop quiet,
jam-packed ballroom. Sitting crossed-legged in the front
row, just a short distance from this guru's feet, I was wedged
between other yogis into a tiny space on the floor, nervous
fingers clasped together in my lap. This was my first full experience with Ma Jaya, before we officially claimed each other
as teacher and student. We were there in a New York City
loft-style event space, twinkle lights threaded overhead, arched

glass windows overlooking the bustling streets below. The room was crammed with hundreds of yogis and eclectic spiritual seekers: a diverse array of seasoned guru devotees comingling with brand-new aspirants. The crowd was bedecked with prayer beads, *chakra* tattoos, and ephemeral scarves, and everyone was abuzz with anticipation and hopeful curiosity.

My boyfriend had met this mesmerizing guru previously and was excited for me to meet her, but I was taken aback by her powerful presence and direct, no-nonsense style. I was not sure Ma was the kind of teacher I wanted. I was happy to sit there quietly and soak it all in, but Jacques couldn't leave it alone. He was a magnanimous, handsome Black man with a rich French African accent. Born and raised in tropical Cameroon, he and I met at a kundalini yoga summer solstice event. Jacques fashioned himself a bit of a lady's man, with lots of pretty, young female students adoring him as they attended his packed NYC yoga classes. He was a talented teacher, blending his own style of yoga with a thoughtful mysticism.

Jacques kept trying to get Ma to notice me, flashing his radiant smile and innocently flirting and joking around with her. I kept jabbing him in the side with one elbow, doing my very best not to be noticed. On his third attempt, Ma turned purposefully toward him and asked that question, shooting a rainbow-colored arrow straight through any toxic masculinity and stopping him dead in his tracks. As he sputtered and squirmed, confused and taken aback, Ma proceeded to banter back and forth with a gay man—a flamboyant, statuesque drag queen, perched regally on a chair at the back of the hall. They volleyed quips about how cute Jacques was and how much fun it would be to see him come out of the closet. Being gay does not diminish one's masculinity, but Ma was provoking Jacques intentionally. Gurus often have an outrageous willingness to use any means necessary to shock a person awake, even when it skirts the line of social propriety. Jacques was reeling. I could feel the heat pouring out of his ears, a cartoon steam tantrum preparing to blow.

I was staring at Ma, falling head over heels, unexpectedly in love. *Damn,* I thought. *She is powerful. There is absolutely nothing on this earth that this man needs more. This is a total ego-check for him. A truly masterful throwdown. A spiritual bullseye splitting open the exact target he needs to bare the most.* It also felt as if Ma was targeting something bigger—piercing any homophobia lurking in the corners of the room.

Jacques was addicted to attention from women, loving their lavish praise and thriving on the feedback. His ego grew compliment by compliment, fangirl by skinny blond fangirl. Sitting next to him during this exchange, I could almost feel his ego shriveling, his arrogance beginning to die. The moment shifted as Ma began leading a magnificently deep meditation, followed by an unnervingly vulnerable question-and-answer session. Suddenly, the event was over, and we spilled out onto the Manhattan streets, a shocking riot of horn-blast in contrast to the thick spiritual quiet we had all just absorbed.

"I don't understand," Jacques exclaimed, with real earnestness. "Why would she do that?"

"They explained it at the beginning," I replied. "It was an ego death, a cutting away of what you do not need, of what keeps you from being free."

At the start of the event, the moderator had gone over Ma's style of liberation work, her Kali-esque ability to see where we are stuck and aim the sword sharp and true. They even cautioned us not to ask her anything unless we were ready to hear an honest answer.

He spun on the sidewalk to stare at me, as if I had now spoken in a foreign tongue. "What?" he screeched, incredulous. "I don't understand! Why would she say that?" The last word emitted a high-pitched squeak. His tenor was rising, the steam escaping. He kept repeating this phrase over and over, during the dark, bumpy ride, clicking across the Brooklyn Bridge to the leafy quiet of the outer boroughs.

## Kali Comes to Call

I had seen Ma briefly in New Mexico as she had received an award the previous summer, but this encounter lit something deep within me. This was the beginning of a real relationship with the goddess Kali, in the form of Ma. Kali is the deity of transformation and truth, who cannot and will not allow falseness to stand. From this moment forward, many things that were not holding true in my life began to unravel. I experienced a profound internal change, a shifting of boundaries, a new stance of self-awareness. I was shedding layers of unworthiness, issues I thought I had already addressed and healed, but this was a much deeper strata of work. It was bone-deep. It was Kali.

*This is the great unlearning that yoga teaches us:*
*we have to let go of the unreal to reveal the real.*

This is the great unlearning that yoga teaches us: we have to let go of the unreal to reveal the real. We have to relinquish unworthiness or arrogance to find genuine self-worth. We have to heal the wounds that would keep us in an "almost" relationship, so we can have a radically meaningful relationship with our own soul.

This moment marked not only the beginning of a true guru relationship between Ma and me—where the teacher helps expose our illusion so we can finally get free of it—it was the beginning of the end of my romantic relationship with Jacques. Even though we became engaged a few months later, our interactions with Ma were far from over. Kali was coming to call.

## Brahmacharya: The Energy Body Teachings

The study of yoga is based on energy: how to use it, how not to, what to do when it awakens like a steamroller and launches you into a meditation that just won't stop. And sexual energy is compelling, naturally vigorous stuff. In their exploration of energy, the *rishis*, the original yogis, studied the energy of the entire cosmos: the stars and the wind, the oceans and the moon, the flora and the fauna, the body and the body of the planets hovering in the night sky. They studied nature to learn about human nature.

In this, they began to explore the conservation of the life force to cultivate a self-discovery process. This may have been the original intent behind *brahmacharya*, which means to walk with God, to create and sustain a profound focus on the sacred energies, pulsing all around and within us. So, the yogis began to restrain themselves from sex and constantly directed potent, practice-infused energy inward and upward. They did this to transcend attachment to the world, to use desire and the creative impulse in a different way: to create yoga—union—with the sacred.

In this way, brahmacharya can be understood as a form of energy management. The idea is that instead of being driven by desire, we can merge it with consciousness. Why would we do that? To experience sustained, instead of temporary, bliss.

## MINI PRACTICE

### CONSCIOUS PRAYER

This is an easy practice to intentionally draw your energy back inside your own body. It is a form of prana, or lifeforce, management. You use the following Conscious Prayer gesture to pull your awareness back inside yourself and center, recalibrate, and align. It creates purposeful awareness and intentional presence.

*Technique*
You can do this practice anytime, anywhere. Drop your hands near your hips, inhale and circle your hands and arms slowly out beside you, then draw them together, palm to palm, at the center of your chest in a Prayer Position. As you do this, gather in your awareness. Gather yourself back to yourself, back to the moment you are in now, drawing your energy into the center of your body. When your hands touch, create centeredness. Exhale with the hands in prayer, establishing a calm awareness. Release the hands and repeat, totaling three times.

## Reluctantly Devoted to You

I was wearing a heavy, gaudy, ruby- and diamond-encrusted engagement ring that was totally not my style. That should have clued me in that this was an ill-fated situation, because when Jacques presented me with the ring, I disliked it immediately. First, I was unprepared, startled that he was asking me. I loved him, I did, and I thought that maybe I wanted to be married… for sure I wanted to be wanted. I wanted to be loved. Though I was not totally convinced, I said "yes" anyway.

But I didn't like that ring. It sounds trite. It sounds shallow. Shouldn't you know what the other person would love to wear every single day, forever, before you buy it? It was a towering confection of glittering red and blazing, oversized, blinding, cushion-cut diamond white. It was flashy, ostentatious, over-the-top, and totally not me.

I felt the weight of this bauble weighing down my hand and my heart. I was sweaty, miserable, and arguing with Jacques as we hiked up a long, slow incline in the Jemez Mountains of New Mexico. It was early morning, and the gleaming desert sun was determined to heat up our already inflamed attitudes, sand eddies swirling across dusty roads, crisscrossing the sage-dotted scrublands.

You could see for miles across the mountain vista, the morning light streaking the broad sky, pink, red, and a soft, southwestern rose brown. We were up high, hiking above the ashram, the tents and outbuildings flashing in the angled sunlight. Brilliant glints of silver off the stream sparkled below us, and our hearts were pounding in the thin air, the high, breath-stealing altitude kicking in during our first days in the desert. We were attending a white tantric meditation retreat, a kundalini partner practice that was radically intimate. Hours on end of eye gazing with your partner, chanting the sacred names of truth and reality, matching breaths, and opening your hearts. Not a good idea when you want to hide from who you are with. Or knock him on the head. It was really, truly, acutely pissing me off. Okay, he was really, truly, acutely pissing me off.

I was beginning to suspect my partner was bypassing some deeper, more delicate inner work and he was, in my grouchy sunburnt opinion, not showing up for it. He was avoiding the intimacy—pretending, posturing. He was behaving in a manipulative, controlling manner rather than having the tough conversations. He was blaming, shaming, wiggly, and subversive—externalizing everything rather than bringing the truth back into his own heart.

As a spiritual teacher, I have assisted many people in doing this work, but it is more difficult when it is your partner, your boyfriend, fiancé, husband, person, love, or beloved. I struggled to maintain compassion. He was a yogi after all, so I expected more. I know that no one likes to feel their own pain. We all avoid our most raw, intense wounds, but I am really good at holding space for people. How could he not show up? How could he show up with a misguided ring instead of his real heart? I was agitated, upset, and blaming him. I was not at my best; neither of us was. Both of us trudged up the mountainside, silently fuming.

As we crested the next big rise, a long, white Cadillac cruised right toward us, stirring a swirling trail of dust. The two of us rose to the top of the hill in tandem with the car, in a cosmic choreography, all players arriving in precise rhythm, our dance effortless and attuned. As the vehicle skidded to a gravelly stop directly at our feet, the automatic, tinted window buzzed slowly down. Black hair and flashing gold jewelry appeared—incredible.

"Namaste!" Ma screeched out across the quiet morning, a yogic salutation of regard. "What the hell are you two doing out here?"

A silent pause, crows cackling in the distance.

"Wait, are you getting married? Are you two engaged?" Another silence, thicker, weightier than the first. "Come to my ashram in Florida and I'll marry you."

Nothing could have shocked me more. I was astonished at her presence here on the outskirts of nowhere. Speechless that she could somehow know of our fragile, improbable betrothal. Ma was pushing on this newly constructed commitment that was barely standing on its own.

We chatted briefly, her turbaned Sikh driver bemused in the front seat. After a stumbling, incomplete promise of a possible marriage or a visit to her southern ashram, the gleaming white Caddy and its message-wielding passenger rolled on up the mountain. Jacques and I began our precarious descent.

### It's Got to Be Real

Our relationship began to unravel immediately as we struggled through a day of partner practice in the relentless intensity of a Kali-infused awareness. One translation of Kali's name is reality, as in "it's got to be real." Ma's assessment of us was insightful and astute. She skillfully touched a place in me infused with uncertainty. Why was I reluctantly engaged to be married? Why was I choosing this? Yes, the Indian leader of the American kundalini yoga tradition was encouraging us to marry—he was old school and arranged marriages were common among his students. But seriously, what was I doing? Why was I saying yes to something that did not honor who each of us was?

By the end of that endless day, driving down out of the mountains, I realized the relationship was not... real enough for me. Or maybe, I was not yet real enough for me. Under a starlit desert sky, over smoky green chile enchiladas, we attempted to resurrect the fragments of our bond, but some things are not meant to be fixed. We agreed to let go of each other. If we weren't going to do the deeper work together, I was going to do it on my own. I chose aloneness over the bondage of a relationship that was not right for either of us. In that choosing, I knew I had an ally, and her name was Ma... or Kali... or Kali Ma. I wasn't really sure.

## Wild Barefoot Celibate Yogini Monk

Let's face it: relationships are hard, messy deep dives into learning how to live with your heart open. And sex is—well, it's complicated, even when it's not. Our sexuality is part of who we are, and if we are using yoga to become whole, no aspect of us can be fragmented or abandoned. Sex is good. It's fun. It's natural, joyful stuff. So why would the yogis, a bunch of nature-loving spiritual seekers, explore and experiment with abstinence? And how is this applicable today? Without sex happening, none of us even exists. Sexual energy is the most potent energy on earth, other than love. It is more immediate, more primal, more... insistent. The plants, bugs, fishes, birds, and animals are all doing it. Pollen rains from the trees, bees hurry across the skies, and turtles cavort in the oceans. People cruise each other, hooking up. Sex is happening all the time.

In the ancient yogic texts, the fourth yama—brahmacharya—appears to espouse celibacy, or at least many traditions interpret it that way. This may be the most controversial and misunderstood of all ten methods outlined in yoga's foundations. All that hubbub may have to do with the power of desire colliding with the power of conscious choice, because each one of us gets to choose how to use our own life.

*Each one of us gets to choose*
*how to use our own life.*

Yogis study prana, the life force within everything. Sexual energy is universal, creative, and wildly powerful. If we are attempting to create transformation—to transform our suffering into consciousness, to transform into the most vibrant, radiant form of ourselves—we are going to need some mighty fuel. If the sexual force has the potential to evolve us through our karmic obstructions, then let's use it.

## Healing Sexual Trauma

The staccato rumble of a motorcycle pack echoed up the driveway, setting my skin crawling. My breath instantly stopped. Bearded, leather-clad bikers spilled off their ragtag Harleys and through our family doors, bringing the greasy, pungent animal smell of unwashed men. My brother's motorcycle gang was made up of rough guys, most of whom seemed nice enough, but that day as I tried to exit the kitchen, I got pinned, then groped in our cedar-scented coat closet. He pushed me face first against the grainy cedar planks. I extended one hand, flailing uselessly, clutching the soft hanging garments. He pawed my breasts, thrusting his pelvis hard against my backside. His booze-and-cigarette stench poured hot across my neck as I struggled to maneuver myself free. He laughed, throaty, against the back of my ear. He was assured of his power, and I was unsure, unformed in mine. As a young teenage girl, this encounter left me feeling wanted and dirty, manhandled and bereft.

Sexual trauma made me feel like the boundaries of my body were not my own. I had a sense of powerlessness around being a sexual creature, but not having agency over how or when I would encounter sex. Countless women can tell a similar story, with different hands abusing them. "Violence against women is endemic in every country and culture, causing harm to millions of women and their families..." said Dr. Tedros Adhanom Ghebreyesus, WHO Director-General. Sexual assault is an abuse of power that often stems from toxic masculinity. Sexual trauma and sexual shame are not exclusive to women—they are all too common in the transgender and LGBTQ community—and straight men, to a lesser degree, have experienced such abuse as well. It is an experience that the yoga community has not escaped.

Over the last decade, a number of male yoga leaders teaching in the US, including two I studied with, have been accused of sexual assault. Some of them have admitted their misconduct and criminal behavior, but many have not (Griswold, 2019). This leaves an unresolved, open wound around sexual misconduct in the yoga community, one we must collectively continue to heal. The brahmacharya teachings can help us heal from such abuses, but the therapeutic process is deeply personal. As community leaders, we can create safe spaces to openly discuss such traumas. We can create sanctuaries. As individuals, we can choose a period of abstinence to safely uncover and gently address these painful wounds. I recommend working with a trauma expert to do this. In recovery from a situation where we felt powerless, doing the brave work of healing can recenter our power within us.

Self-chosen abstinence is not about avoiding our sexual nature. It is about understanding and befriending our sexual truth. We can intentionally use creative power to heal our relationship with our bodies and with sex. There is nothing inherently shameful about us. Shameful acts that are done by us or to us, however, need to be healed. The idea of our own sexual energy as sacred places authority firmly inside us. We can embrace ourselves in sexual complexity to remember and embody sexual simplicity. I couldn't control the biker who grabbed me that day in my family home, but I do have the power to heal myself from that encounter.

After that experience of adolescent powerlessness, I found solace in the yoga practices, relief in the meditations, and embodiment in the breathwork. I leaned into my burgeoning asana practice, flowing from pose to pose, but I could barely touch the feelings at that time without wanting to run. I was young and new to yoga's healing potential. As an adult, I eventually found my way into addressing sexual trauma, purging abusive touch from my body, and releasing the inevitable shame that accompanies such abuse. I used the tools I share in this book to witness, grieve, heal, and forgive. To fully embrace ourselves and our freedom, trauma of any kind must be lovingly released.

## Sexual Shame and Gender Fluidity

Many LGBTQ folks have experienced a distinct kind of sexual shame or trauma in the name of God or spirit when they were told there was something wrong with them or that they would suffer greatly because of their sexual truths. Many have experienced exorcisms or forced conversions. This is tragic. No one gets to dictate how you express yourself in the world. Your self-expression is your true song, a song that includes your body, mind, and soul. In my inclusive mindfulness community, I have witnessed many people come out of the closet to claim themselves as LGBTQ. I have watched in quiet wonder as folks realized they were transgender, then found the courage to live as themselves.

In a recent conversation, Jacoby Ballard, author of *A Queer Dharma,* shared, "Swami, being in your Atlanta yoga community as my gender identity was unfurling was really powerful for me. It allowed me to find and be my true self and relax into the process. It gave me time and space to understand my sexuality in a place that didn't judge me or tell me how to be." Jacoby went on to explain, "Some interpretations of brahmacharya can reinforce shame, especially for someone queer. If we go into a spiritual community and it states that sexuality is not welcome, we never get the opportunity to explore who we are. It's important for queer people to be empowered and self-determined in their sexuality. When we are held and valued in spiritual spaces—like the one you have created—we can heal, connect, love, and realign. Then sexual shame no longer holds us back because we know that we are loved."

I believe that if you are gender fluid or LGBTQ, God made you that way—you are not a mistake. God must have been having a really good day when She created such gorgeous diversity, unleashing Her own divine creativity into the world.

## The Deepest Relationship of Your Life

Brahmacharya is about deepening your relationship with yourself as yourself—without selfishness. It is prioritizing the higher self, the higher mind, even a higher spiritual vibration. Brahmacharya asks you to pour yourself fully into your spiritual evolution and liberation. In many traditions, this includes a monk-style abstinence from sexual activity, which any of us can choose. For a modern yogi, it can provide a means of using the intense, wild powerhouse of sexual desire to get curious, to question how to utilize the potent firestorm of sexual urgency to explore a deeper connection to the sacred, and to wonder about harnessing and directing this energy upward to create such a profound soul bond that it leads to embodied liberation.

The yogis of old observed that it took a lot of energy to move through entrenched patterns of negative behavior or belief. They realized it took a vigorous, energetic focus to create ecstasy and bliss, which was what they were after. Yogis were the original bliss junkies.

*Yogis were the original bliss junkies.*

They turned toward the most potent human energy they could find: the creative force. Like scientists harnessing the cellular energy of atomics, they questioned... What happens if we don't use sexual energy to get off, but use it as fuel to create union in a different way? The feeling of genuine oneness has to be bigger than the ecstasy of orgasm or sex, or who is going to try it? Living mostly in the Himalayas, the rishis and sages were immersed in the verdant beauty of nature. They studied their relationship with the earth, the rivers, the sun, the animals, and the planets. They grew food and observed how directing energy in plants could make the plants grow stronger or weaker. Like any good gardener, they learned that if you cut off some buds, your fruit grows sturdier elsewhere. Same with animal husbandry—if you redirected sexual energy, the animal would behave differently. The yogis observed this intentional use of creative energy and applied this science to themselves.

Brahmacharya is often described as celibacy or sexual moderation, but a more nuanced meaning is to remain in steady, focused contact with your own soul. To listen so deeply to the sacred essence that is being expressed through you, that you can share that unique expression with the world, whether you are having sex or not.

Yogis also observed how much time and energy it takes to be in a successful marriage, to raise children, and to provide for a family. Choosing brahmacharya can have us choosing the sacred as our primary love relationship. However, we have all seen what happens when celibacy is imposed, not chosen, and it's not pretty. Sexual desire is potent and dedicated celibacy is a spiritually mature decision not to be made lightly. It's a choice to be made from the inside out, not the outside in. If you have chosen celibacy and it isn't working for you, it can become a crucible of shame, which is the exact opposite of yoga. If you feel one way and behave another, that's duality. It's anti-yoga. It's creating a rift within yourself where none need exist.

Understanding this personal choice is paramount: in the modern-day, interfaith, nondenominational teachings of yoga, the use of your energy and life force is totally up to you. Most people love having sex—why judge that? You can be a celibate yogi. You can be a polyamorous yogi. You can be a monogamous yogi, a divorced yogi, a tree-hugging, free-floating, sometimes-single, sometimes-partnered yogi. But the yogis would have you ask: If sexual energy is the power behind creation, what happens if you use it in a way that is not about creating babies? Or orgasms? It's the most powerful force that we know, so can we use it for our own evolution? Or to connect to a sacred reality? Does ecstatic spiritual experience really happen, and can we recreate it for ourselves?

*Does ecstatic spiritual experience really happen, and can we recreate it for ourselves?*

## Spiritual Enough Already

I was hustling though the Atlanta airport, chatting on the phone with my sister, on my way to another out-of-town yoga and meditation training, when, exasperated, she said to me, "Geez, where are you going this time? Aren't you spiritual enough already?"

Befuddled, I paused and thought, "What does that even mean? Is that really possible? Can you be too spiritual?"

I couldn't get enough of yoga and meditation. It was making me stronger and freer than I believed possible, given what my sister and I were born into. I was enthralled. I was practicing yoga, breathwork, and meditation with a focused intensity and I just couldn't—or wouldn't—stop. I had found an effective tool to scrape off the thick karmic detritus of our upbringing. Honing these skills was creating so much transcendent revolution, there was no way I was going to pull back now.

But never in a million years would I have guessed that I would choose to be celibate. That was the potency of encountering a real shakti teaching. I was stripping away old layers of unworthiness at an astonishing rate, experiencing a white-knuckled acceleration of transformation, getting totally high on being alive, and sustaining bliss, love, and spiritual expansion through it all.

I became celibate without totally meaning to. I thought I would try it out for a little while and see what could happen. No vows, no grandiose declarations. Just a joyful little yogi, feeling her way into being, every day. I experienced radical healing. I was doing what some of those dusty yogic texts prescribed: awakening kundalini, the lifeforce at the base of the spine, and moving it up to merge with the sacred. It felt crazy and wild. I was blissed-out on meditation and I absolutely loved it. I felt like a conduit of love, shakti, and spiritual force. People were flocking to my classes because I had the juice, and I was willing to use it and chastely share it to get us all spiritually juiced.

If I had known I was going to be having sex for the last time for a minute—which turned into my last time having sex for a couple decades—I would have gone another round. Wait... really? No, I wouldn't have, because the appeal was gone. The magnetism was missing. Love was an essential part of sex for me, and if it was wavering, so was the attraction. You know how you can perceive your partner as the total package, until you don't? And then you can't? That happened. As much as my now ex-fiancé needed to look at his attention-seeking-for-validation trait, I needed to turn back to myself to unearth self-worth from within. I needed to be alone for a bit. So, I leaned into the unknown, into the mystery of learning how to be alone—like all the way, really alone.

### Intentional Aloneness

Choosing a defined period of celibacy can be healing. If we take ourselves off the apps and away from the dating scene, we free up considerable time and energy. This vitality then becomes an integral part of evolution and transformation. Being open and inquisitive about what works for us makes life, love, and the pursuit of happiness a lot more fun. Stripped of shaming, we are empowered to choose.

*This is why yoga is a living, breathing art.*

This is why yoga is a living, breathing art. It's juicy. It's not made to be stagnant, fixed, or rigidly prescribed. It's meant to meet us where we are and empower us to simply be more ourselves, walking through the world with sacred reality right by our side.

## DEEP PRACTICE

---

### FULL MOON PRACTICE FOR SINGLES OR COUPLES

On each full moon, do a meditation and set an intention to feel attuned to the rhythms of your body and the rhythms of the planets. Do this outside under the full moon when you can.

*Technique*
- Place one hand over the center of your chest and one hand over your lower abdomen.

---

- Inhale deeply. Chant the Sanskrit mantra *"Om Namah Chandra,"* drawing out the words to use up all your breath. "Om Namah Chandra" means "I invoke the energy, the sacred consciousness of the moon."
- Repeat this mantra twelve times, once for each month, or moon cycle.
- Then inhale and imagine pulling lunar energy up from the base of your spine to the third eye, the meditative focal point between your eyebrows. Picture an image of the full moon at the third eye.
- Meditate on this image for a few minutes, feeling reflective, cool, and centered.

## DEEP PRACTICE 2

### FULL MOON, FULL HEART RELATIONSHIP PRACTICE

In the following practice, we explore restraint and conservation of sexual energy, a yogic teaching based in tantra. This practice is intended to be sweet and mutual, so both partners can hold each other—and the relationship—in high regard.

Here's the basic idea: for partners to make love on the full moon—only on the full moon.

This practice is intended for couples interested in exploring and intentionally using sexual energy.

First, it provides ample room for anticipation, which is important in long-term relationships. Teasing, flirtation, courtship, and seduction are core components in creating relationships that last. Next, the practice creates neither overindulgence nor excessive restriction, and can be modified to twice a month or some application that works for that individual couple. Last, it works with the energy of the earth, the push and pull of the moon and the tides, the rising and falling, waxing and waning, attuning us to our own natural circadian rhythms. It lets us dance with the rhythm of desire. Brahmacharya is ultimately about attunement: being finely attuned to the energy of the sacred, in yourself, your partner, and the universe around you.

You and your partner need genuine intimacy to talk about sex and to clearly convey your boundaries and needs while also listening attentively and openly to theirs. In this case, you are attempting to make sex more rare and special. This is imperative because lots of people carry unnecessary shame around sex and desire, which is not the point. If anything about this practice creates weirdness, excessive tension, or unworthiness, opt out. No shame or judgment should arise, just good, clear communication and connection. No one is prescribing anything to you; you are creating an intentional practice together.

### Technique
Exploring the Full Moon, Full Heart Practice together is about getting closer, not further apart.

- **Clear Desire:** To explore this technique and its effectiveness in enhancing your relationship, initiate a clear, loving conversation with your partner about your desire level and theirs. Be willing to stretch your ideas about need and desire and play with it, finding what works for your partnership. Choose whether to explore this practice together. Discuss what creates joy. Joy can be about listening, cuddling, and creating deep heart connection—and wholesome anticipation. This means being loving in myriad ways that are not solely about sex.
- **Active Admiration:** Tell your partner what you love and admire about them, which is always a good idea in relationship, especially if you get caught in toxic familiarity, or the inability to look at your partner through the eyes of love. It can be difficult to see your mate as sexy when they won't clean the bathroom. Admire them. Say what you love about them out loud, often.
- **Intimacy Parameters:** Agree on your parameters together. Choose a number of times per month for "nights of intimacy," like once, twice, three times per month. If it's a lot more than that, you might not want to explore this practice just yet. You may already have a cadence to intimacy that works well. Choose a timeframe for how long you want to experiment with this practice, like three months, so that you go through three full moon cycles together.
- **Awaiting the Full Moon:** Make a date, preferably on the full moon. As the date gets closer, you may

want to flirt, tease, plan, create anticipation, and
seduce. Then just go for it. See if this enriches the
intimacy in the relationship. Also notice if you
feel more attuned to the rhythm of the moon, the
rhythm of your partner, and the rhythm of your
own body.

# 5
## LOVE
## ANYWAY

**Aparigraha:** (uh-PAR-EE-grah-HAH)
detachment, non-greediness

*"Letting go gives us freedom, and freedom is the only
condition for happiness. If, in our heart, we still cling
to anger, anxiety, or possessions, we cannot be free."*
THICH NHAT HANH

## Longing and Belonging

I did not love the Catholic mass. As a child, I didn't really
understand it. No matter how many times the priest intoned
that the pale, lifeless wafer turns to flesh, all I ever saw, felt, or
tasted was the wafer. The priests were promising mysticism,
but I hadn't experienced it.

Although I didn't like going to mass, I loved being inside
the vast, stone church. The quiet, sacred space was calming
and comforting. Plus, at eight years old, I was wild about
the incense, the bells, the stained-glass images, and the art.
I loved the soaring ceilings, the bloody crucifix, the polished
ebony wood. I was mad for the statues, the holy relics, and

the swish of dark black robes. I thought of the church as a sanctuary, a place of refuge—as promised. It was something safe, something good, something to uplift our spirit.

So, I was startled by the spirit-quashing conversation I had with the head of our small Catholic diocese.

To my young mind, Father Niedergeses was extremely old, ancient even—slow as Christmas, trundling down the aisle—but he was kind. He and I were sitting together in the smooth hardwood pews in the nave of the church, sunlight streaming through colored windows, peace surrounding us. Having grown up around the rituals and pageantry of Catholicism, I longed to take part and do what the other kids were doing. I wanted to ring the bells, to light and snuff the beeswax candles. I wanted to solemnly follow the priests. I wanted to wear the small, draped outfits that mimicked the vestments of the holy men. I was filled with curiosity about the phenomenal world around me, but I was even more curious about the subtle realm of the sacred.

"Father, I would like to be an altar boy... err, an alter girl," I asked, nervously.

He turned, pivoting in the pew next to me. "Girls cannot be altar boys," Father Niedergeses said in a heavy nasal voice, tinged with a slight German accent. He paused.

"It cannot be. You are a girl," he said, a little more decisively.

Judgment had been passed, and I was out. His dismissal embossed a spiritual discord upon me, one that my upbringing had prepped me for, but that I hadn't fully understood. I was told no, you are not good enough. You do not belong. Those were not his exact words—as I said, he was a kind man—but that's what I heard. Part of the church was reserved for the better gender and that was final. The result was a contraction of spirit in me, a religious confusion, and a piercing sense of separation. My gender was something I had no control over, yet it was confining me, defining me as not belonging. I felt shame for asking, for thinking I could do it, for not "knowing my place."

Catholicism was all the spirituality I had been exposed to, all I had access to. I was relentlessly bored by daily religion class, watching it slowly beat the juice out of a once-vibrant tradition, one nun-droned lecture at a time. Now the priest's refusal slammed a spiritual door closed and locked it tight. I didn't belong to Catholicism; it didn't belong to me. I would always be seen as lesser by this tradition because of gender. Because of gender, I was already seen as lesser by my family.

What was this boy's club that I was being excluded from? What was mysticism if it didn't celebrate us all? Could girls and women belong spiritually? I was struggling to find my place in the world, a place of real belonging. I needed a spiritual "yes."

> *One of yoga's definitions of*
> *aparigraha—detachment—is*
> *unconditional love.*

### Wholeness Without Attachment

One of yoga's definitions of *aparigraha*—detachment—is unconditional love. This appealed to me because it indicated I would be accepted regardless of gender. It sounded like a spiritual "yes." At fourteen years old, I swiped a yoga book from my oldest sister and started doing the practices. The book outlined a twenty-eight-day course, and I immediately repeated all twenty-eight days three consecutive times. Each time I practiced, I experienced something new, a sensation of resonant well-being. Each meditation walked me past my daily thoughts and into a reservoir of quiet inside myself. I would practice and get closer to peace. Wasn't this what spirituality was supposed to offer?

The teachings of yoga were my first encounter with a sacred tradition that was not dictated by a religion. Catholicism made me feel isolated and alone, which I already felt in my family. Yet here was yoga, taught as an achievable pathway, a practical toolkit to wholeness, for men and women, boys and girls. Could this be a way back to myself? An opening?

Plus, most of the images in the yoga book I had nicked were of women—doing postures, meditating, demonstrating breaths, all without judgment or shame.

As I began to delve further into the deep and simple practice of meditation, I realized I wanted something. I was attached. I had an agenda. I wanted the spiritual promises to be real. I wanted to heighten my relationship with spirit, with my inner self, with nature, and with love. I didn't want God to exist only in a church or only for men in robes.

I wanted to be touched by the sacred, to be truly moved, held, and broken open by love. I wanted a living experience of something I did not yet have language for. I wanted the union, the wholeness, the connection. I didn't understand it yet, but I wanted yoga—to be merged with sacred awareness.

## Aparigraha: Losing Control on Purpose

Often when we love, we hold too tightly. I definitely do. I love having my people close, connecting deeply, and loving full throttle. *Aparigraha*, the last of yoga's five yamas, or disciplines, means detachment and non-possessiveness. The Sanskrit word *graha* means to grab, to cling, to clutch, like a greedy fist wrapped around a yearned-for possession. Grasping at love never works, but our fears often drive us to do so. We become entangled in attachment when we hate being left out, when we have abandonment issues, or when we relish the illusion of control. When we can pry our fingers off the people we love and instead love with an open hand and an open heart, we allow ourselves a superior expression of love: love infused with trust.

*Detachment is not indifference.*

Detachment is not indifference. It is a form of love where the heart is open—wildly, outrageously open—which expands our heart's aptitude. Indifference is laced with callousness, self-preservation, closed heartedness, and a lack of caring. Indifference also permeates us with the inability to be vulnerable or to connect deeply. Detachment, on the other hand, teaches us to let go of what we are not and find a freer, more genuine version of ourselves. We love and let go simultaneously. It is not either/or. Detachment will help us release resentment, forgive the small stuff, keep our hearts open, and lovingly work on the big stuff.

## Don't Touch My Feet

We tiptoed into the dank interior of a crumbling New Delhi temple, uncertain if Westerners were welcome, peering around the ancient door. The peeling paint of the old wooden panel was woven through with embedded metal scrollwork.

Its surface was patterned with incredible intricacy, a braille work of message rough and uneven under my hands. The door was heavy, misaligned, and reluctant. It felt as if it had been there since forever; I could feel its immense history pushing back against me. The panel squealed slowly open, signaling our arrival in the main hall of the ashram temple. After decades of yogic study and practice, I was finally in yoga's birthplace: India.

I had landed in the sprawling metropolis of New Delhi. I was flooded with anticipation and then utterly flattened by culture shock. I knew India would be wild, but the streets were electric with vibrant, deafening dissonance: the sheer volume of people coupled with the olfactory overload of incense, rotting fruit, and deep-fried curry oil merging with an almost viscous, ever-present stench of air pollution.

The crushing disarray of cars, lorries, buses, cows, bicycles, wagons, camels, motorcycles, putt-putts, donkey carts, and rickshaws was unnerving. Attempting to cross any major street was almost unmanageable, even when a charming, wizened grandma who stood less than five feet tall had us take hold of her fluttering, neon green sari scarf, and guided us gently through the mayhem.

Jangled, energized, and insatiably curious, we—my two traveling companions and I—ventured forth. We planned to get out of the cacophony of the city as soon as possible, to explore the northern provinces, the Himalayas, various ashrams, elephant refuges, monkey temples, and holy sites. But since we were in the historic city of Delhi for a few days, we went exploring.

One afternoon, overfull from a lunch of spicy *aloo gobi*, handmade *chapatis*, and fragrant chai, we stumbled into a small suburban ashram on the outskirts of the massive city. Dedicated to the Indian saint Neem Karoli Baba, the "grandfather guru" of my yoga lineage—in other words, my guru's guru. Maharaji, as Baba is known, is renowned for his outrageous love and generosity of heart. He is Ram Das's, Bhagavan Das's, even Steve Jobs's guru. I had read about, heard stories of, and sat listening enthralled to numerous people's experiences with this legendary teacher of teachers. I was walking in a place I knew Maharaji had walked. I could almost feel his presence, hear the echo of his laughter, and connect to his never-ending flow of love. I was excited, thrilled even, to join with the origins of my tradition and finally see yoga through the lens—the incredible kaleidoscope—of India.

### The Long Arm of the Patriarchy

My companions were a married couple, a man and a woman. We had attended many of life's richest rituals and moments together—they were true friends and *gurubai*, or a spiritual family of sorts.

Sliding off our shoes at the entryway—an Eastern practice of respectful regard—we tottered, barefoot but reverent, across the cool marble floor of the wide hall. As we approached the center of the open space, an elevated altar became visible with an orange-clad swami sitting perched at the edge of the marble dais, skinny legs peeking out from under his *dhoti*—a type of sarong—feet dangling like a child's, barely grazing the floor. He was thin with long, bushy silver-and-white-streaked hair, a wispy mustache, and a brown wizened face accustomed to India's hot sun. He sat peacefully, eyeing us as we approached, his arthritic hands together in *pranam*, a prayerful greeting of honor and welcome. I was eager to meet my first swami from Baba's order, feeling that we too were gurubai, that we belonged loosely to the same spiritual family. Like meeting an unmet cousin, you greet, welcome, and open to them because you feel kinship, a sense of belonging to each other and to the same clan.

In India, and in the yogic tradition, when you meet an esteemed elder, teacher, or holy person, you touch their feet as a sign of humility and reverence. They have walked the earth longer than you, accumulating experience, so with this gesture you acknowledge their wisdom and relinquish your own ego or pride. You, in turn, are blessed by them, given a simple benediction.

On this day, my cohorts ushered me forward to greet the native swami first, since several years prior to this trip, I had also been ordained as a swami. As I bowed before him, feeling the sacred significance of this moment, I reached my bare hand toward his bare feet, reaching for connection. He immediately pulled his foot away. Startled, I looked up into his eyes and he shook his head no. Not understanding, I drew my hand back, felt my heart contract, stood unsteadily, and shuffled backward. My male friend stepped forward, not having fully seen what had just taken place. He too bowed, reached to touch the holy man's feet and was warmly greeted, allowed, embraced even.

*Aha,* I thought, belatedly, *I recognize this. The long arm of the patriarchy.* It reaches into, around, and behind women all the time. Blatant sexism was greeting me in another house of God. And here I thought I'd found a tradition that escaped it.

## Distance, Denial, Indifference or Detachment

I was confused, insulted, and demoralized, just like I was at eight years old when I was rejected as an altar girl by the Catholic priest. I placed my hand on my female companion's arm to keep her from approaching the swami and being snubbed in a similar way. Then I thought of yoga's toolkit and settled on aparigraha, or detachment, to help me reflect on this situation. A passage from the *Bhagavad Gita* sprang to mind:

> *"All your thoughts, all your actions, all your fears and*
> *disappointments, offer them to me, clear-hearted; know*
> *them all as passing visions.*
> *Thus, you free yourself from bondage, from both good*
> *and evil karma; through your detachment, you embody*
> *me, in utter freedom."*

I had spent the better part of my life studying and living, applying and delving into a spiritual teaching that I naively thought was void of sexist dogma. I had already studied with two separate male Indian gurus, both later accused of sexual misconduct and abuse of power, so I had some idea of the patriarchal belief system that placed men over women in India. However, over decades, I had poured myself into the liberation lessons of yoga and gained more freedom and empowerment than I ever thought possible. Over the years, I had recognized Ma Jaya as my guru and had embraced Kali as a powerful deity, so sexism in yoga didn't touch me personally as much anymore. My steadfast practice of the yogic disciplines remained strong because they worked, and you can't really argue with results. These extraordinary ancient tools facilitated the discharge of my self-limiting beliefs each and every time I practiced. Anguished, I would begin a session. Recalibrated, rearranged, and released, I would emerge. The practices were indeed empowering me, even if the male leaders weren't. They were teaching me detachment from my "thoughts, actions, fears, and disappointments."

Here I stood, having traveled halfway across the globe, disappointed and disenchanted by this wild-haired Indian swami. However, I do have rose-colored glasses; they are one of my superpowers. I see the good in people. I want the good to win. I believe in love and kindness, and the man before me was a devotee of these principles.

Assuming the swami was trained to believe that women are less than men, I found myself feeling a little bit sorry for him. Who would teach him? How would he grow beyond this limiting, culturally inherited belief in gender inequality? He unknowingly had just taught me a great lesson in detachment. Even if he—a revered swami in a gorgeous tradition—could not see my value and worth, I could. Even if he could not see equality in all, I, a female, American-born swami, could. I believe we are all made up of love, and if we use love as a foundation of equality, we can heal ourselves and the world.

## I Can Only Be Happy If...

If aparigraha means non-possessiveness and detachment, let's look at what attributes possessiveness and attachment create. Attachments are typically based in fear, insecurity, control, or unworthiness. We fear being alone, so we cling too tightly. We are afraid of stillness or silence, so we rush to fill the void. We have benefited from a hierarchy, so we fight to preserve it. We believe we need another person, job, car, experience, or compliment to be okay. We habitually place our self-worth outside of ourselves. We think, "I can only be happy if..." instead of realizing that we can choose to be happy, no matter what.

When self-worth resides within us, we are okay, even when we get affronted or hurt. It's not that we don't enjoy external validation and wholesome connection with other people—of course we do—but we don't crumble or rage if everyone doesn't love us, honor us, or hold us in high esteem. We stabilize by centering our worth inside ourselves. We are already okay; we just have to remember that we are. If I cannot stand in my worth as a swami pulls his foot away from my respectful female hand, my worth has been placed outside me, in his hands. Now I am attached to his opinion of me!

*Detachment teaches us to be present*

*with any thought, feeling or experience*

*without getting hooked.*

Detachment teaches us to be present with any thought, feeling, or experience without getting hooked. It teaches us to open to what we experience while we avoid clinging or indifference.

Detachment helps us untangle the stories we tell ourselves that obscure the truth of our lovability. If I cling to that moment with the Indian swami, I will make up all kinds of nonsense to reinforce my unworthiness. If I can sit with it, open to it, feel the pain in it, learn from it, forgive it, and release it, I am detached. In that detachment, I am free.

## Forgiveness as a Freedom Tool

On that day in India, I went outside and sat in the ashram gardens, connecting to my inner worth, unshackling myself from the stories my self-righteous mind wanted to weave around the experience. I sat, I felt, I understood, and I let go.

A few moments later, a manager of the place came to chat with me about their new herd of cows. I was moved by his beaming pride and simplicity. He was so happy to be able to feed the village children through the daily ritual of milking the sweet-faced cows and making fresh yogurt. This kindly connection with him also recentered me, reminding me that when we embody aparigraha, we transcend greed and ego by reducing our wants to needs and living simply and softly on the earth. Those kids were living pretty simply, and so was this joyful caretaker. What need did I have here? I didn't need validation from the swami. I wouldn't wake up hungry the next day, like many of the children. I, too, could be simple. If I choose to forgive this hurt, I am free of it. If I cling to it, I am bound to it.

*In the radical act of forgiveness,*

*I expand my perception—*

*of myself and my relationship with the world.*

In the radical act of forgiveness, I expand my perception—of myself and my relationship with the world. I can choose attachment and suffering, or I can choose detachment and freedom.

## Detachment as Embodied Freedom

The ancient yogic text, the *Bhagavad Gita*, outlines one of the world's foremost teachings on detachment. It states that doing the right thing for its own sake, without concern for success or failure, is the surest way to embody freedom.

With detachment, we can expand our ability to open more expansively when we face a significant loss in our life Instead of closing down around our broken heartedness. We can learn to use heartbreak to break us open to more love. When our heart does break—and since we are human, we know it will—that break creates a crack, and if we can open, breathe, and trust, we can feel love pouring through that fissure. We can love and open, love and open. We can ask love to break our heart wide open—and in this vastness, we can love anyway.

## MINI PRACTICE

### FORGIVENESS MEDITATION

Forgiveness teaches us detachment from our pain, not as avoidance, but as release, so we do not cling to our wounds. This layered practice is done in three phases, addressing suffering on various levels. If you touch deep woundedness while doing this practice, allow yourself time and space to feel what you feel with the intention to heal it.

*Technique*
Sit for meditation. Be present. Feel your body and the space around you. Relax and close your eyes. Trust yourself as you learn the art of forgiveness.

Read the following statements aloud, one sentence at a time, giving yourself time after each sentence to feel it. You can also read each sentence aloud, then repeat it silently once or twice, like a brief mantra, giving it time to sink in.

**Part One:** Say: "There are many ways I have hurt and harmed others. I have caused suffering out of my own pain, anger and hurt, or out of misunderstanding. I feel the sorrow of having hurt, betrayed, or abandoned others. I feel what I still carry from this. In this moment, I ask for forgiveness. Please forgive me. May I be forgiven. Let my heart be willing to ask for forgiveness. I am open and I receive it. I am forgiven."

**Part Two:** Say: "Just as I have caused pain, hurt, and suffering to others, so too have I hurt myself. I have betrayed others or myself and abandoned my own integrity and love. I feel all the ways I have caused suffering to myself. I remember and feel the broken heartedness from this and allow myself to be present with it. In this moment I offer myself forgiveness. I offer myself tenderness and kindness for my own humanity. I forgive myself for making mistakes. I feel compassion and forgiveness for myself."

**Part Three:** Say: "There are many ways others have hurt and harmed me. Every one of us has been hurt. We have all been betrayed. I feel the sorrows I still carry from this pain. I feel the many ways others have hurt, betrayed, or abandoned me. I feel this now. To the extent that I am ready, I forgive you who have hurt me. I offer you empathy and I release you. I will not carry the pain of hating you in my heart. As much as I am able today, I forgive you."

End with a deep breath, filling yourself with expansive love. Feel the spaciousness where you released long-held hurt or resentment and purposefully feel the balm of forgiveness.

## You Don't Know What's Going On

In the late 1980s, Bruce lay dying in his tiny Inman Park apartment. For Gerry and me, the metronome of Bruce's gasping breaths laid the soundtrack to his last days. Gerry and I had become great friends and allies as we stitched together a patchwork of death-midwifery—weaving a tight bond across the many fatalities we experienced as the AIDS epidemic raged on. An offshoot of my contemplative arts for HIV+ classes at Grady Hospital was a ragtag care team of dedicated volunteers, willing to do laundry, pick up groceries, or take trips to the pharmacy. We bought chubby tubs of Ben & Jerry's to soothe aching throats. We dusted glittery knickknacks for 6'8" OCD drag queens without blinking an eye. But by Bruce's third round of going on hospice, even the hospice nurses were stretched to the limit. So, we decided to try riding it out at his home.

Bruce moaned, unconscious, wrestling with his demons, and suffering the insurmountable pain of bodily transition.

Gerry and I would take turns being with Bruce, but as our dear friend's life drew to a close, we both stayed. After days of thinking we were arriving at Bruce's last breath, it was nearing midnight, when Bruce's breath slowed, like it does as death approaches. It stayed slow, excruciatingly slow, for hours.

A handsome, blue-eyed blond, Bruce worked out religiously, the epitome of a hot-bodied, sculpted gay man. He was kind and sarcastic and panicked at the thought of wasting all those hard-earned muscles away. Bruce was conceited, but he carried it well, and with those rippling biceps, he deserved a little flash and preening. Those days, if you "went on hospice" it meant you were dying and that you were entering your last weeks or days. It meant come and say goodbye, gather the party, do not delay, get on it, and get on it now.

Bruce, however, went on hospice three separate times over the course of one year. Every time his worn, dwindled body seemed ready to go, he would rally and return to us, a little wearier, but tearfully, laughingly willing to embrace life again. He would walk right up to death's breath-rattling door, pause with one hand spread wide against the onslaught and somehow willfully pivot, turning his back on death once again. Bruce slowly rekindled his awareness, indigo eyes peeking open, unbelieving that we were all still sharing the space and the place where death walked. Bruce was released from hospice over and over again, to return home where his two sleek Siamese cats sat patiently, tails twitching, awaiting their father's return.

Gerry and I had walked enough people through the dying process to be open to assisting his death at home. He and I were both students of Ma Jaya, having benefited from her endless compassion delivered with insightful humor and timeless wisdom. Ma had an AIDS respite adjacent to her ashram and had been doing this work for much longer than either of us.

The sun came up. The sun went back down. Night fell, and darkness descended softly all around us, enveloping the room in a blue-gray hush. Nearing midnight, we entered into a grimy delirium. Gerry and I hit our collective wall at the exact same moment. We both stood and locked eyes across Bruce's ravaged body, his breath coming once every few minutes for unrelenting hours. We bolted out of the room and cruised straight out of the second-story apartment onto a tiny wrought iron landing precariously suspended out over the edge of a dark parking lot.

I snagged the cordless phone off its cradle on my way out the door, clicking the retractable antennae slowly up as I went. We perched on Bruce's miniature balcony while cicadas echoed across the hot pavement and the summer smell of freshly mown grass filled the night. We looked at each other as I dialed Ma's number.

"We have to speak with Ma," I blurted into the phone, hands shaking.

This was pushy, unprecedented behavior, since bossing around your spiritual teacher is mostly not done. "Tell her Bruce is dying. Again. And we are freaking out up here."

After endless minutes of muffled voices, phones covered with sweaty hands, Gerry and I squeezed together, practically pushing each other off the minute ledge, desperate to hear some words of guidance. Our perspiration-streaked faces smashed together, both trying to hear the sound of her voice. I thought for one hilarious moment we could be kissing or falling or laughing or dying. We were all of it and none of it, grasping onto each other's presence in the hot August night. All I wanted was for someone—not us—to know what to do. Bruce had experienced more suffering than I ever thought possible.

Ma's voice came crackling to life on the phone, Brooklyn pouring thick and heavy through the line.

"Tell me, my girl, my love," she said, "tell me what's happening."

Gerry and I tried to explain, but our words roiled together, spilling out our sorrow and fear, our witnessing of endless hours of misery. Our words bled over each other in a profusion of pent-up, relentless pain as we stood in the potency of the moment and our inadequacy in meeting it.

"He keeps dying and not dying, dying and not dying. How can it be like this? How can he be made to suffer so much?" I asked. My anguish for his anguish, my beautiful blue-eyed boy.

"Jaya Devi. You don't know what's going on," Ma said slowly.

"Exactly! I don't know what's going on! Help me, Ma! How can it keep happening like this?"

"Jaya Devi. You don't know what's going on," Ma said a little louder, gathering momentum.

I paused. I tried to understand.

"Jaya Devi!" Ma almost shouted, "You don't know what's going on." This time it landed like a slap, the kind you need when you are spinning recklessly, weak-kneed into sobbing hysteria.

"Oh! Oh, wait! I don't know what's going on? I don't know what's going on!"

The light of detachment flicked on distantly in the recesses of my mind.

I did not know what was going on. I am not in charge of when Bruce dies. I am not in charge of how Bruce dies. I am not the boss of death. What was I thinking? I am not the boss of anything!

I was flooded with a palpable relief. I was here to bear witness, to love, to hold Bruce's gaunt hand—no matter what. Ma's words were like the pinprick of reality that popped my exhausted mind, letting it fall back into what was real. Like an overinflated party balloon—pow—then buzzing haphazardly around the room, my mind gasped out its tired head of overly responsible steam. I do not know what's going on. Oh, thank God. What a relief.

Ma explained about the *bardo*, the place in between, the gap. In the space between life and death, a lot can occur. It's a potent, mysterious space, a space where we don't really understand what's happening. She talked about karmic resolution, about healing trauma, soothing unfinished relationships, and easing old emotional wounds. She said this is a space where you never want to insert yourself. Some people stay here for days or weeks or years. With some people, they're done with this space in an instant. But you don't decide anyone else's trajectory or how much suffering they can bear. You just show up and love.

Bruce died just before dawn the following morning, easing out on a rasping shudder of release. With the sun slowly rising, Gerry and I cried until we could barely stand, hawking out grief and bone-weary sorrow. We had seen too many deaths, too many breaths not taken. The love could crack you in two if you weren't careful. I was learning how to let my heart break while cleaving myself to love at the same time. I was bowing to death as he stalked through the room, knowing death could teach me something about life and love and impermanence, about how love—the unconditional love of detachment—was the only permanent thing.

## Not the Boss of Death

We are not the boss of life. We are certainly not the boss of death. We have to learn to relinquish control and open to what life is teaching us. I was young and death was terrifying to me, yet I had somehow, inadvertently, opened myself to learning from the most intense part of life: death. Ironically, becoming a student of death taught me to become a student of life and of love.

In the *Katha Upanishad*, the young protagonist seeks out Yama, the god of death, and asks death to be his spiritual teacher. Ultimately, Yama teaches him that fear and attachment will limit you to a life half lived—a life spent chasing the senses—and understanding this can free you. Once you let go, you can be lovingly detached and trust that life and death will embrace you, teach you, and evolve you. You trust that the sacred wildness of being—and not being—is all part of the dance.

*You trust that the sacred wildness of being— and not being—is all part of the dance.*

I was learning to honor the wildness of loving anyway, of living double since Bruce wouldn't get to continue living, of loving even when it feels too hard. In every interaction, no matter how painful or joyful, if I choose love, I am there, in love. Each time my heart breaks, I breathe my way into awareness and I choose love. I hold love. I bow to love. I surrender to love. I become love.

Finally, I learn to trust, even in death: I am loved, and I am love. Then the mystery takes hold, and in the moment of death, love rides out on the last breath, the soul reunited with its source, the source of love. I am, we are, we have always been, and always will be. We are not clinging—just being... love.

## DEEP PRACTICE

### KALI'S KARMIC RESOLUTION

In the Karmic Resolution Practice, we explore the concept of detachment as unconditional love. Instead of clinging, you love expansively. By honing this skill, you free yourself and others from the too-tight bonds of need. This can illuminate, heal, and deepen your bond in close relationships: with partners, loved ones, family, and friends.

This bold practice creates the experience of aparigraha, loving detachment. Detachment as unconditional love means you can love without saying "You have to be this way for me to love you." Aparigraha enables you to choose freedom from the negative patterns that bind you—the patterns you repeat over and over that cause you suffering. For example, why do you choose similar relationships with similar partners who have similar issues, causing you similar heartbreak? These are your karmic patterns, the ones with roots, the ones that take focused intention to release.

This practice is beneficial to do with each of your parents, partners, siblings, and children. Include your more challenging relationships, those where you hold resentment or feel unresolved tension or conflict. You can also use this technique with employers, colleagues, coworkers, or neighbors with the intention to heal rifts or arguments and create a more peaceful, detached way of being in the world.

The Karmic Resolution Practice has a profound effect, so I recommend doing it in a specified time-frame. Create a safe container, and then use it to do deep work, especially if you are addressing trauma. This practice can excavate unresolved wounds or resentments, so create a compassionate receptacle of time to hold this work. Choose a time to do this every day for three to seven days. Commit to it as a daily appointment and clear the space to do it each day. It can be done morning or evening, really any time of day, but dredging up old pain is fruitless if you don't give yourself room to process and heal.

In this practice, I use the image of Kali, the goddess of transformation, who you have already met in this book. You could use any sacred image or concept: the Christ, the Buddha, the unembodied force of light and love—any representative of the good. Simply substitute your sacred beloved's name or image for Kali's. I use Kali because she is a goddess that resonates with me but also because she embodies utter freedom and carries the sword of detachment. The tantric goddesses are powerful shakti energies who have been adored and worked with since the beginning of time. Lovingly, respectfully invoking Kali for this work is remarkably effective because she is a powerhouse. She does not mess around. But if you invite her in, remember to ask her to leave at the end of each practice session because... she does not mess around.

*Technique*

Sit and close your eyes. Set a *sankalpa,* or sacred intention, for the highest good for everyone. Ask for protection and resolution, depth and kindness, love and extraordinary healing. Ask to work on the level of the soul for all involved. Ask Kali to influence this practice and to teach you true detachment, which is love with no strings attached. Request her presence and open to her energetically. Create a sacred feeling where you can trust you are safe.

Invite the person you are working with into this sacred space. See or feel them before you. Imagine and sense cords of energy emanating from you to them and them to you. These are the cords of relationship, the energetic lines of attachment. Notice the physical location in your body where these strands of energy are rooted. Now ask for Kali's divine assistance. She represents transformation, so respect that. Now ask permission to put your hand on Kali's sword-wielding hand. Together, cut the cords. You may feel a release, a severing, or an unhooking. Your work now is to let go of the tendrils of entanglement and attachment. You release them to release you.

Repeat this affirmation: "I release you. I offer our relationship to the Universe."

Repeat it until you feel an internal change. You may feel the shift right away or it may take longer. This profound inner work creates pranic—energetic—healing on the deepest level. Feel the open spaces within where the entanglements once lived. Let yourself feel changed.

Now wash yourself with the prana, or the vital energy, of pure love. Imagine a pranic swirl pouring softly down from above, like a hazy vortex of light. Wash away any threads of attachment or neediness. Feel the open spaces within yourself healing and being soothed with compassion, empathy, and kind regard.

Offer gratitude to Kali for the sacred assistance, then respectfully ask her to depart.

Feel love for the other person, void of the attachments. Just love. Love the other person fully as you let go of the past. Don't try to fix or heal them, trust the universe to do that. Ask for karmic resolution, for the highest good in the relationship, for healthy connections infused with openhearted detachment and unconditional love.

# 6
# POLISHING THE RADIANCE WITHIN

**Saucha:** (SOW-chuh) purity, cleanliness,
sacredness, simplicity

*"I will not let anyone walk through my mind with their
dirty feet."*

MAHATMA GANDHI

## Who Is a Yogi?

The drums reverberated, filling the meditation hall, the tempo steadily rising. The room was vibrating, a sacred chant ramping up, lifting hearts and voices, anticipation pulsing in time with the beat. As our first Classical Yoga Teacher Training's graduation ceremony commenced, the drumbeat accelerated. Trainees perched excitedly around the room, moving with the rhythm, ready to be honored as the radiant teachers they had become.

We were an eclectic bunch, including musicians, artists, teachers, and skydiving instructors, a Persian engineer, a gay hairdresser, a horse massage therapist, and a psychologist from a remote mountain region of India. This happy array of seekers poured themselves into studying, learning, sharing, and practicing. They drank in these profound wisdom teachings, which now lived inside each of them. They studied various poses until their bodies were sore. They practiced lengthy meditations until their minds were sore. They demonstrated, taught, and articulated. They practiced mudras and chanted mantras, learning ancient ways to direct energy. They had used all these practices to polish themselves into readiness. They were lit up, proud of their accomplishment, and excited to graduate.

A few years earlier, in the mid-1990s, I had founded a nonprofit sacred center, based in the teachings of yoga, meditation, and community service in Atlanta, the heart of the American South. I was searching for teachers to fill out our roster, those interested in creating a distinct, welcoming yoga community that could be an urban refuge. This was before the avalanche of 200-hour teacher trainings erupted onto the Western yoga scene, before there was a yoga studio on every corner or an array of body-enhancing yoga classes at your local gym. Most American yogis at that time were focused solely on the physical. It was difficult to find well-rounded teachers who had studied the rich philosophy of yoga.

Teaching the spiritual magnitude of yoga is not nearly as sensational or profitable as the bendy body stuff. However, these simple wisdom tools can aid anyone in any type of body. In a recent conversation with Daniel Simpson, the scholarly British author of *The Truth of Yoga*, he shared his exhaustive research on the early yoga texts. Simpson found that while people enjoy stretching, "It was very clear that for most of its history, yoga was about sitting and meditating— with a bit of breath control—but it was certainly not about doing contortions, in sequences, on yoga mats, in rooms, in between stressful jobs. It was much deeper than that. It was all about solving this whole problem of being me."

With this depth in mind, I created an accredited 200-hour teacher training—jam-packed with a rigorous investigation of all eight limbs of the classical yoga path—and this crew was about to complete the course.

One of the upcoming graduates was a Black woman who has cerebral palsy and uses a wheelchair. She is as deep a human being as I have ever met. Her disability makes the physical practice difficult for her, but she is a yogi. Her intention, willingness, and commitment have her merging with the moment over and over again. That merge is yoga—union with reality—where we learn to be fully, genuinely present. Everybody can do this no matter how flexible or how stiff they are. The only real flexibility yoga requires is the flexibility of our minds.

As the ceremony commenced, I invited her to roll up and graduate first, placing the *mala*, the honorific garland over her head. She holds the distinction of being the first of hundreds of teachers that have completed this richly faceted course and the first of many marginalized graduates. The room erupted in applause and celebration. Everybody, bendy or not, got it. They understood what it meant for her to be seen and honored in this way. It was clear—crystal clear—to all of us what a yogi is and who yoga is for.

## Saucha: Polishing the Lens

*Saucha*, the first of the five niyamas, translates as purity, cleanliness, sacredness, or holiness. The basic idea behind saucha is this: if we are organized and tidy, if we live simple and clean, life is easier. Things flow. The mind is complex, but the soul is simple. A clean, clear space supports a clean, clear mind, which in turn supports a clean, clear life.

In many ways, saucha is about simplicity: simplifying our needs, purifying our environments, and clarifying our minds. Saucha instructs us to clean the kitchen, bathe regularly, and wear clean clothes. Yet, saucha is not about avoiding the messiness of life. It is about addressing and transforming clutter and confusion. In its deeper dimensions, saucha advises us to clean up ignorance, ego, attachment, aversion, and fear—which is the work of a lifetime.

### You Are Not Impure

Many people, including those in the LGBTQ, BIPOC, or non-Christian communities, were taught by dogmatic religious tradition that there is something inherently impure about them being themselves.

*The purification practices of saucha do not imply that you yourself are somehow impure...*

The purification practices of saucha do not imply that you yourself are somehow impure, but that some habits, spaces, closets, behaviors, or thoughts may benefit from a more methodical scrub. Rather than ask someone to conform to a limited idea of correctness based on gender, religion, sexual orientation, age, ability, or skin color, saucha asks us to purify our ignorance through nonjudgmental acceptance and wonder. When we meet people who are different from us, we can become curious about who they are. We can learn about their experience and widen our scope so we can embrace the incredible variety in the world around us.

In studying saucha, we also see an intersection of *ayurveda*, the science of life, and yoga, the union of being whole. These two sister sciences evolved out of India's rich spiritual tapestry and were part of the traditional yogi's purification practices. Saucha creates clarity by polishing the body, emotions, and mind—purging out toxic experiences, beliefs, and behaviors. For example, if you have been a victim of misogyny, homophobia, or racism, the saucha teachings can help you heal the wound. Saucha asks us to be patient and present, to create spaciousness in our households as well as spaciousness around our heartbreak. We do this to get clarity and to witness our chaos or suffering with compassion. We create clear space and allow love to come in.

## Laying It All Down, Then Stomping on It for Good Measure

I was lying on my back on a hard wooden table, saturated head-to-toe in oil. I was immersed in an ayurvedic *pancha-karma* retreat, an immersive set of ancient purification rituals designed to cleanse the stuffing out of you on a cellular level. Staying at a funky lodge in the quiet of the Colorado mountains, I began this transformative work with my friend and colleague, Dr. John Douillard. John has a simple, earthy clinic and his style of treatment is an all-natural, everything goes, herbal immersion. John is masterful in these traditional healing arts, and I was immediately submerged in a four-hand massage, steam and ice, skin scrubbing, hair pulling, head standing, back bending, fire breathing, and ginger-imbued nostril clearing.

Having dedicated my life to learning and living the teachings of yoga, this was one more step, taking me further onto the path. Entering the rustic center each morning, the spicy-sweet aroma of the day's concoctions would greet me: a bubbling brew of roots, leaves, oil, and spices simmering in a hot pot next to the massage table. As I opened the door to the sunny treatment room, I shivered in anticipation. This monk-like retreat is done in total silence—the yogi's practice of *mauna*, or silent retreat—except for occasional meetings and disconcertingly intimate pulse readings with John.

In the quiet of the center, John is a dynamic hustle bustle of focused intent. He is an esteemed expert at ayurvedic pulse reading, which is a healing art unto itself. When a highly trained practitioner like John listens to what is working inside you—and what isn't—it's transformative. This act of deep witnessing creates a safe space for extraordinary levels of purging and healing.

Dr. John would sit and curl his long fingers around my wrist and listen for three, sometimes four, even five minutes. He would listen like he was hearing the sound of the cosmos pulsing through my veins. John had a way of attuning himself deeply to the rhythms of my body and soul. I felt incredibly seen, known, and observed. I loved it, and it was totally unnerving. I leaned into the work.

I remembered that letting go of old trauma can happen in so many ways and that healing takes place in many different venues: on a cleanse, on a meditation cushion, on a yoga mat, even in the sacredness of not-doing, just being or being fully seen. Healing can happen in a current of anger, as you hurl eggs at a wall. It can happen on the edge of a Colorado mountain range as you excavate crusty, old patterns that still have roots in you. It can happen in a simple moment of intentional release when habits are disrupted by solitude, care, and willingness.

### Stomping on It for Good Measure

One day during the healing retreat, my irritation was bubbling to the surface, the hot jolt of anger flashing through me. I was incredulous at my continued self-doubt, frustrated with the tedium of self-healing. I was detoxing my emotional body and irritated by the sheer intensity of feeling. As I strolled back to my room on a narrow, worn footpath, I cut through a field where the prairie dogs live. The path overlooks the Colorado Flatirons with their strikingly dramatic, angular sandstone forms. Sunlight flashed through the moving clouds, shining down onto the sunbathing prairie dogs, as they craned their whiskery faces out of their little hill-homes. The wind cut long swaths across the parched grass.

Dead, oversized leaves, curled like fists, drifted across the field in the blustery autumn wind. I stomped on one, pounding it into a puff of brittle gray leaf dust. Stomping out my frustration, I wanted the old patterns to just... go. The stomping felt excellent, like an adjunct therapy to all this cleansing. I stomped another leaf-fist, crunching it underfoot, clomping out a primitive release. Stomp, release. Stomp, release. I felt the repetition of action, the satisfaction of destruction, the symbolism of crushing my anguish to dust. The stomping ritual created a gratifying discharge of inner debris. Stomp, release. The prairie dogs, having none of it, leaped back into their holes.

Feeling satisfied, freer, I headed back to my quarters to decide whether I wanted to take my upcoming monks vows. My skin was yellow from turmeric scrubs, my tongue was yellow from liver purging, and my brain was yellow from bellowing out old transgressions. One definition of a *sanyassin* or swami is "one who lays it all down." My ultimate questions for myself became: *What if I laid down everything—all my insecurities and attachments—and placed my life in the goddess Kali's hands?*

*What if I claimed myself only as love?* This thought reawakened a centered calmness, a trust in who I am. This was my choice. I was stepping further onto the path of devotion, healing as I went, allowing the obstacles to fall like ash in the wind. Healing happens in a simple moment of understanding, when we finally just let go. I reawakened a trust in who I was, who I had always been, and who I always would be.

*This is saucha: clearing out the past to find the present, the simplicity to just be.*

This is saucha: clearing out the past to find the present, the simplicity to just be. Away from all the doing, I settled. I turned toward the resounding quiet, and my relationship with the sacred energy of the universe rushed forward. It bowled me over. I recognized the wild reality of the cosmos and I breathed it in. I recognized myself without all the extraneous stuff and held out my hands, opening them to the sky. In the letting go, the cleansing, I returned to myself. I returned to simplicity.

## Kali: The Wild Wisdom Goddess

Ayurveda uses oil to treat almost everything that ails you. On this panchakarma retreat, warm aromatic elixirs were poured into just about every orifice of my body: oil in my ears, eyes, nose, and mouth. I experienced nightly herbalized oil enemas after a monthlong mono diet of mung beans and rice, oil rubbed into my skin until I glistened like a baby seal, oil saturating my long, thick, soon-to-be-shaved-off hair, staining my pillows and dripping down my smooth slick back. Soothing streams of oil drizzled over my third eye for a seemingly endless absorption that led to startling mental quietude and a visitation of the Black mother Kali.

As the warm stream of oil dripped relentlessly onto my forehead, I had a vision, an abrupt moment of clarity, of seeing with my eyes closed, a tangible knowing. It started as a pulsation, a soft image dancing on the inside of my forehead at my third eye—the meditative focal point between the eyebrows. Like a movie flickering to life, projected onto the screen of my mind, my third eye flashed open. I was blinded by an image of Kali, the wild tantric goddess who embodies radical transformation. The image was clear and unexpected. I have been immersed in many moments of pure peace in meditation, but this graphic explosion was completely new. It wasn't a thought; it was a living reality, imprinting itself across my mind. It felt like an actual knowing of her, both intoxicating and intimidating.

Ayurveda asks us to be deeply observant: to align ourselves with nature and use all-natural methods to clear out anything keeping us stuck or unhappy. *Panchakarma* means five actions, five purifications, five karmic releases. This is concentrated, yogi-style cleansing. It isn't easy, but it is effective, sometimes alarmingly so. I needed it *now* because I was desperately searching for clarity. I was on the cusp of being ordained as a swami, in an unorthodox lineage that embraces female monks. With a grand public commitment ceremony just a few short weeks away, I was questioning if I was on the right path. My closest friend, who was already a swami, had suddenly departed the order in a dramatic flourish, heightening my unease. I needed some time for deep reflection to see if this commitment felt viscerally true for me.

The goddess Kali is my beloved of beloveds, my unnerving resting place, my *ishta devata*—the sacred image-essence that rings truest for me. She is a tantric wisdom goddess who wields the sword of compassionate detachment with utter abandon, ready to cut away our falseness to reveal our truth. She wears a garland of skulls to warn us: our attachments must die. With her gorgeous ebony-black skin, she cuts away the familiar so we can leap wildly into the unknown. She works relentlessly on our behalf. Her power is unmistakable. With her in my corner, transformation was coming for me. It was inevitable.

## MINI PRACTICE

### POLISHING THE CHANNELS

You don't have to go on a panchakarma retreat to reap the benefits of this ancient wisdom. A multitude of easy, daily efforts are effective. One of the simplest, *ushnodaka*, is as uncomplicated as sipping warm or hot water throughout the day.

This humble practice stimulates the flow of lymphatic fluid to keep your immunity vibrant and strong. It is designed to open the channels of elimination, so you can let go on all levels. It is a thorough hydration practice that Dr. John Douillard prescribes regularly, because a hydrated body works better, sleeps better, fights off viruses better, and just feels better.

### Technique
Sip hot or warm water hourly, or at least three times during the day, taking a few good slurps each time. Use hot water if your body runs cold, warm water if you tend to run hot. You can sip heated water as often as you like, but keep after it until you feel your body shift into a physical sense of satiation.

This thorough hydration remedy accelerates the removal of toxins from your body, polishing the channels. It is highly recommended during the cold winter months. Use a timer to really get into it, sipping every twenty minutes, especially anytime you feel compromised—jetlagged, catching a cold, burned out, hungover, or just plain exhausted. I employ this replenishing wellness tool frequently, using a thermos or insulated coffee mug to keep my daily dose hot.

## Just Go For the Ride

Yoga has been an oral tradition for eons, personally handed down from teacher to student, and as you dive further into its intricacy, you understand why. It's complex. It's nuanced.

It reveals unhealed issues and catalyzes personal change. Practiced in its fullness, yoga picks you up by the ankles and shakes out what you need to release, like a cartoon bandit, jiggling out all your loose emotional change. It is beneficial to have an ally when you have been turned upside down and left to grope about in unexplored territory. It is comforting to have a trusted guide nearby, holding a lantern, lighting your way as you search through the dark unknown of who you are becoming.

My first guides were books. Tucked away in my 1970s shag-carpeted bedroom, I devoured everything yoga-related I could find: first, the classics like *Siddartha*, the *Upanishads*, and the *Bhagavad Gita*. These readings were soul poetry—touching, but not quite quenching my unspoken inner thirst. I had a few of the yoga manuals of that time, full of faded black-and-white photos of very thin women in tight leotards doing pretzel-y poses. I repeated the guidelines in all these yoga books—doing meditation, breathwork, and all the postures, adopting an attitude of loving kindness, and attempting openhearted presence. To go further, I would need a teacher.

When I moved to Atlanta in my early twenties, I was excited to seek out my first real teacher. Donna DeLuca had recently opened a small, light-filled yoga studio in a drafty storefront space. The eclectic, intown studio vibe was just right for an artistic yoga-seeker like me. I loved Donna's hybrid *vinyasa* classes—poses linked, like a dance, in a continuous flow—and felt an immediate connection with her and her teaching style. She was deep and funny, mystical and irreverent, a lovely blend of the spiritual and the earthy. She and her husband ran the place with the charm and ease of a hands-on, family-run, heartfelt enterprise.

Yoga was affecting me deeply. It was instigating authentic healing, and every time I practiced, I felt better, but the practices were often frustratingly hard. I wasn't a naturally flexible yogi. Sometimes I couldn't do the poses or I didn't like the sensation a posture provoked. Deep backbends opened my belly and solar plexus into an elongated vulnerability. The disorienting tilt of a headstand reminded me that my world had always been a bit upside down. I started taking as many classes as I could, because even if the shift was subtle, every single session, I emerged less stressed and more attuned.

This, too, is saucha, the purification of practice. The asanas—the physical poses of yoga—wring you out. They bend, open, strengthen, and stretch you in ways you didn't know you needed. Even if you feel you are not very adept, the postures provide terrific relief from daily tension. The poses meet you where you are—there is always an easier pose and always a harder one. These ancient practices began changing me, and I was leaning in because I had never grown like this before.

*These ancient practices were changing me,*
*but I was leaning in because I had never grown*
*like this before.*

Donna told me my kundalini was rising, my evolution was unfolding, supported by my dedicated practice. She was witnessing my fast-paced growth and encouraged me to trust it, trust myself, explore everything that was revealed and to go all in. This was phenomenal guidance. The practices kept clearing me out, even when I didn't understand how they were doing this exactly. Yoga practice works on many levels—the physical, the emotional, and the spiritual—and we do not always comprehend how this growth is happening. We just feel it and go with it, which is okay. I showed up and did the work and felt the impact of all of it, just as every book, scripture, and teacher instructed budding yogis to do.

During this time, I was also in art school, pursuing a BFA. I was doing all the things creative college students do: running around with boys, drinking, sometimes to excess, in the boisterous, meet-everyone-in-the-bar manner of my Irish family. I was studying, making art, living my bohemian life, but falling in love—hard—with yoga.

## This Champagne is Bringing Me Down

I lifted a slender flute of sparkling pale beverage, the crystal flashing in the setting sunlight, watching the effervescence rise against the glass, escaping in their festive bubble-dance. The newly married couple kissed. The crowd applauded. But as soon as the cool, crisp liquid slid down my throat and started to enter my bloodstream, I felt a deflation, a sense of coming down, a bodily collapse of my natural high. I slowly became aware of something profound. An inner shift was occurring. I found myself standing in a group of revelers, laughing, when suddenly I thought, "This champagne is bringing me down. It's ruining my buzz."

The purpose of indulging is to feel better, right? To uplift and enjoy, to release and relax. To expand and open into a more joyful space than where one began. But in that celebratory moment I realized imbibing this magical substance was not elevating me the way it once had. It was bringing me down instead of lifting me up. It was making me feel less open and alive, instead of more. I stood in wonder, reassessing. I asked myself, *"Is this also saucha, the inner distillation of yoga's deeper practices?"* In that moment I realized that yoga was both uplifting me and ruining me. Either that or it was saving my life.

I come from a long, illustrious line of drinkers—imbibers, rowdy, life-of-the-party celebrators. I love rejoicing and connecting with people. However, the elevation of practice had lifted me beyond a line of well-being, until using substances had started to bum me out, deflating my baseline of everyday joy. Over a few months I had observed this buzzkill effect slowly evolving, but the wedding toast moment clarified it for me. I just wasn't entirely sure I wanted to be so clear.

This new sensation felt unique. It awakened my insatiable curiosity. Yogis, including modern yogis, use themselves as their own laboratory of health and happiness. We look at our habits of everyday living and ask: What practices do I choose that make me feel more alive? Or less alive? What increases my joy? What makes me sad or irritable? What clouds and what clarifies me?

Saucha suggests cleaning up your daily habits, separating yourself from any learned detrimental behaviors, to see yourself more clearly. For myself, I decided to put that fizzy champagne glass down and explore life without imbibing for a while. It felt like a new adventure and a bold, decisive clarification of selfhood. What would happen if I enrolled myself as a pattern-breaker for my family and turned away from substance use? Even if I wasn't abusing alcohol, that heavy, generations-old addictive pattern was lurking in my DNA.

As if deadweight was wrapped around my anklebones, I felt shackled to the choices of my forebears, my family, and even my younger self. With a decisive click, I set the light flute on the table and felt clearly what I was up against. I was breaking history apart. In this pivotal moment, I would do something to expand myself, without doing something to contract myself at the same time. I made an unprecedented choice: unblocking, unshackling, undoing. To become whole, I have to stop choosing behaviors that perpetuate my own fragmentation.

*To become whole, I have to stop choosing behaviors that perpetuate my own fragmentation.*

I was learning by unlearning. If I stop clipping my own wings, how far can I fly?

## This Messy, Perfect, Messy, Perfect Life

For many years, I longed to visit India. The home of yoga held a spiritual resonance for me, like a knowing that tickled the dark recesses of my mind. It awakened something not quite remembered, not quite conscious, but just out of my grasp. I listened to stories of yogis tramping around the Himalayan foothills, searching for a mystical connection, a guru, an experience of the sacred that would rock them back on their thickly calloused heels. I had read about India, been deeply influenced by it, and heard trials and tribulations from enthusiastic world travelers. I soaked up anecdotes from my Indian teachers, told in lyrical tones. All shared a reverence for their beloved homeland, which they described as a spice-scented, tiger-and-elephant-inhabited utopia of *sadhus*, saints, and curries.

So, when I arrived in New Delhi, I was ready. I exited the plane with fellow yogis, all bone-weary from the overseas, country-hopping flight. An Indian friend, Kimti, would be meeting us just outside the airport, having invited us to visit him in his home. All we had to do was wheel our carry-on luggage to the appointed place. It was 4:30 a.m. Delhi time, and the vast airport was teeming with bleary passengers. We pushed through the heavy glass doors that led to the outdoor rotunda for pickup and drop-off. Traffic was four lanes deep, horns blaring, rickshaw bikes, motorcycles, and putt-putts vying for space between ox carts and a solitary, anemic camel.

Glancing up at the sky, I was trying to comprehend how it could be glowing a sickly yellow at four o'clock in the morning when the chest-striking, eye-burning, nostril-searing stench of motor exhaust hit. New Delhi, at the time, was the most polluted city on earth. I feared I would not get a deep breath for the coming month, in the country whose wisdom teachings taught me everything about the powers of deep breathing. Our host had mixed up the arrival time, so we spent our first hours in this magical land on a grimy curb outside an urban airport, haggling with cab drivers in poorly attempted Hindi and gasping for breath.

We finally settled into the back of a cab, hoping to be delivered to the correct address. Speeding down a dimly lit, seemingly lane-less highway, a free-for-all of vehicles racing and lurching about, we were flying past a foreign landscape of indistinguishable shapes. I squinted through the cab window to glimpse our surroundings. My jaw dropped open as I realized the towering ghostly silhouettes lining the roadway were mounds of trash, creating a barrier that loomed in both directions, as far as the eye could see. As we hurtled through a tunnel of plastic refuse, higher than the concrete embankments, my idealistic India bubble was punctured once again. Travel is always a revelation. Travel in India would begin with the lessons of saucha.

## Just Hop Over the Poop

We immersed into daily life in India with our magnanimous host. We visited his neighborhood temple, chanting sacred songs. We bargained for mangoes with the local fruit seller as he rode his bike down the lane, hawking his daily wares. We watched housekeepers meticulously sweep and decorate their front stoops every day, using colorful flower petals to create intricate, swirling patterns. We hung out with the elders in the local square, hearing stories, gossip, and mischief, because everywhere in the world, folks congregate, laugh, and chat. We bonded with Kimti's family over tangy homemade meals served with fresh hot bread straight off the griddle.

India is a land of startling contrasts and simple lessons. A few days later, walking with our host in Delhi's posh Connaught Place neighborhood, I found myself casually hopping over a rivulet of open sewage. In a flash, I realized the Eastern act of reverentially removing shoes at the entryway to any home or temple was based in practicality—and another bubble burst. After only a few days, my traveling shoes were revolting, but I was starting to enjoy these revelations. Yoga is lived. It's mystical but also practical. Saucha means cleanliness and purity and wherever you are, cleanliness creates reverence. Whether we are joyfully partaking in the wild cacophony of the Hindu Holi celebration or navigating the poop, camels, and plastic, life is messy, abundant, and reverent. It's not one or the other. It's both.

As Buddhist teacher Thich Nhat Hanh says: "No mud, no lotus." Saucha tutors us to use the mud to grow the lotus. In other words, we intentionally use life's challenges as opportunities to evolve, which helps us blossom into our radiance. These practices can range from adopting a clean simple diet, to purging excess material goods, to uncluttering our minds with meditation.

*Saucha teaches us to see sacredness commingling with untidy, imperfect humanness.*

Saucha teaches us to see sacredness commingling with untidy, imperfect humanness. By striking a balance between the revered and the profane, we walk the middle path of wholeness, embracing the mess, internally and externally, and cleaning it up, wholeheartedly, over and over again.

## DEEP PRACTICE

### SOOTHING SELF CARE WARM OIL MASSAGE

*Abhyanga*, or herbalized oil massage, is a powerful ritual of loving your own body, exactly as it is. You massage warm, scented oil into your entire body before or after bathing, which actually makes your skin glow. As one of saucha's purification practices, warm oil massage improves circulation, aids detoxification, and calms the nervous system. It is a great practice to get you grounded after flying overseas.

Abhyanga has been done for thousands of years to maintain health and balance. It is an excellent way to overcome anxiety, fear, or stress as you calm frazzled nerve endings directly under your skin. The comforting weight of the oil creates a soothing, restorative self-care practice, calms your mind, and imparts deep personal compassion.

## Gather

- Sesame oil, coconut oil, or ghee.
- Any optional skin-friendly essential oils like lavender, brahmi, rose, or ylang-ylang.
- A large old towel that can get oil on it.

## Technique

- Heat a small jar or squeeze bottle of oil or ghee by placing it in a cup of very hot water. Add essential oil drops to the oil if you like. Plain oil is amazing; the added scent is optional, but yummy.
- Spread a large old towel on the floor of your bathroom where no drafts occur.
- Apply a skim coat of warm oil to your body, until all of your body is covered. You can skip or include the soles of your feet and scalp, but the soles of the feet and scalp contain many nerve endings, so coating them with oil increases the calming, restorative effect. Be cautious not to slip or fall with oily feet.

- Once you are completely covered in oil, begin the massage on the soles of your feet, rubbing with your hands and thumbs in long, deep strokes. Continue up your body, rubbing every inch with seven to ten strokes. Use long strokes on the long bones and circular strokes on the joints or organs. Massage your whole body, being loving, patient, and kind. Avoid negative self-talk. The whole massage can take about ten to twenty minutes, but it's a practice in self-love—let it feel like that.
- Use the towel to remove the oil from the soles of your feet before standing or walking.
- Get into a warm/hot shower or bath, which will facilitate the oil's penetration deeper into the tissues. Don't use soap, or use very little, allowing the oil to remain on your skin. If you oiled your scalp, use shampoo or leave the oil in for a glorious hair treatment. Your skin will feel luminous and soft, your mind calm and settled.

### A Modern Yogi's Note on Speed-Abhyanga

In our speed-obsessed world, you may not have time for all this nurturing self-love, but you might need the grounding, hydrating quality of the oil. Abhyanga can be done daily, and in today's world it is necessary, even if it's just this speedy version. Skim coat yourself with oil before or after your shower—quick and easy!

# 7
# THE FIRETENDER
# OF THE HEART

**Tapas:** (tuh-puhs) discipline, to generate
heat and light

*"One must seek the shortest way and the fastest means
to get back home—to turn the spark within into a blaze,
to be merged in, and to identify with that greater fire
which ignited the spark."*

BHAGAWAN NITYANANDA

## Snakes on a Plane of Existence

I was hovering in the in-between, that lovely tranquil state
where you are not quite awake but not quite asleep. After
finishing a gorgeously deep meditation that I did not want
to end, I stumbled down the stairs and pushed open the
heavy wooden front door. It was just past dawn, the sky still
lightening in the distance, the tall grass tumbled over, wet
with sparkling dew. I was meeting two friends for an early
morning walk before the south Florida weather got untenable.
The temperature was already nearing ninety degrees, and my

light cotton T-shirt was promptly soaked through. I slid my bare feet into the flimsy orange flip-flops on the front stoop and clopped over to the sprawling back lawn to meet them.

Wearing shorts to ward off the oppressive humidity, I was upright but not altogether present, unable to shake off the softness of my introspective state. I was feeling both here and there, in the world while gently detached from it, everything a little gauzy, augmented by the early morning haze.

My friends, both meditators, were content and contemplative as well, and after greetings and coffee-scented hugs we ambled along the ashram grounds, watching the bunnies dart in and out of the underbrush. The three of us were artists and yogis and we sauntered along in silence, welcoming the morning with no hurry, just an easy acceptance of starting the daylight hours together.

Walking three abreast on a wide swath of path, my friend Shanti was to my left, a balding monk friend to my right. We were discussing his latest pottery project when a disconcerting sensation broke my quietly mystical reverie. Something was on me. Wait, what? Something was on me, on my long bare leg.

I looked down at a long, fat black snake as it made its circular way up my leg toward the rim of my very short shorts. At first, I wasn't sure it was real. But as that crawling sensation continued and I felt the slithery warmth of a body moving on my body, I was quickly becoming sure—very sure—that this was real. I stood perfectly still, surprised by this unexpected reality, and quite uncertain how to proceed. What is the proper protocol when a snake gets on you?

My two companions had walked a step or two ahead and turned to see why I had halted. Shanti screamed—a full-on hysterical shriek—and ran completely away from me as fast as she could, a total you-are-on-your-own-with-this sprint.

The monk and I pivoted heads toward each other, eyes locked. I was speechless. I mean, my realities were colliding: the sweet nectar of morning meditation was crashing into a chubby, exuberant snake, its black-red tongue flickering and head now hovering dangerously near the hem of my shorts.

I was more startled than scared; somewhere, in the recesses of my mind, I knew black snakes were hefty but not poisonous. I felt the symbolism of *kundalini* rising, entwined with an encounter with nature, which has always been a source of sacred connection for me. The energy of kundalini is said to rise, often symbolized as a snake rising up the spine, an energetic awakening that all yogis must realize.

But this snake, this sensation—this was a moment of being fully present and embodying the yogic art of non-reaction. You know, like, just let a snake, a very big, fat black snake, get on you, encompassing your whole leg, because, um, why not? I had been feeling floaty, gently aloft in my own body, but this got me grounded and awake in a hurry. This got my full attention.

"Lift your leg; let's see what happens," the monk suggested quietly next to me.

Standing on one foot, yogi-style, I raised my left leg, the coils of plump serpent wrapped around it, still spiraling, roving ever upward. With my arms outflung to the side, balancing, breathing, unbelieving, I watched as the snake began to release me, seeking the earth again, extending his elongated neck searchingly back toward the ground. I relaxed as he meandered, then whumped down off my body and back onto the dusty earthen path. No harm, no foul. Reality—in a pretty intense way—had banged into my liminal reverie.

We laughed, shook our heads, and said, "Wow, the darndest things," as the snake slithered off into the underbrush.

Shrugging our shoulders in the warmth of the morning sun, we wandered down the path to find Shanti.

Whose name means peace.

## Tapas: The Art of Non-Reaction

A snake curling itself on my body may be an extreme situation to learn the art of non-reaction, but here's the idea: when we react, we often make situations harder. If lions are chasing you, run. If city buses are hurtling toward you, jump out of the way. Those are wise, lifesaving reactions, and a bigger reaction may have been warranted with the snake. But losing it and screaming at your boss, your friends, your kids, or your partner often exacerbates an already loaded situation. When we pause and practice the art of non-reaction, we open to the space between our reactivity and our deeper selves and create *tapas*.

Tapas is the second of the niyamas. Often translated as discipline, tapas is the friction—the spiritual heat of transformation—that we pursue through embodied practice. Tapas is kindled when we spark an inner flame, almost like rubbing two sticks together in our psyche. We create this heat when we commit to a regular yoga practice—challenging our bodies into new shapes, postures, and explorations. We create this heat when we commit to a regular meditation practice—challenging our minds to accept the discipline of steady self-observation. We create this heat when we commit to a regular kindness practice—choosing loving presence when it would be easier to blame someone else for our suffering. Tapas is the art of intentionally generating internal heat and light.

For example, we create tapas when we hold a breath out for just a moment beyond comfort, not forcing, but extending, exploring. Friction. We practice tapas when we restrict ourselves from an all-too-common habit, like my custom of eating dark chocolate after lunch, every day. Friction. When we restrict our coping mechanisms, we deprive the ego—the dissatisfied, demanding aspect of our mind—which creates a spiritual heat, burning out the familiar pattern of habituated coping. Friction.

When we react to the chronic demands of our ego, we fuel it. When we fight it, run from it, or repress it, we fuel it. But when we open, stay present, and act with discipline combined with love, we ignite a fire of choice. We choose to grow. We create a loving space for transformation to occur. The longer we explore that moment of friction—craving but not responding to the craving in the way we always have—the more we can create positive change.

*The longer we explore that moment of friction—craving but not responding to the craving in the way we always have—the more we can create positive change.*

The deeper dimensions of tapas ask us to burn out our entrenched issues, the ones that are harder to shake. These are the ideas or behaviors that keep us a little bit numb, a little too removed from the transformative fire. Instead of a reaction to a random snake, these teachings ask us to address the unhealed habits of everyday neglect. These are habits like drinking too much or never turning off the TV. These habits keep us from our soul work. When we address these, our inner fire, the radiance of our inner light, can no longer be obscured by mundane activity, nor by any darkness, not even the shadow of our own wounds. We create an arena where we willingly face ourselves and our shadow habits as we heal, grow, and transform. This is how we intentionally use tapas to burn out what is no longer true about us.

What burns in the fire of tapas? It's our ego, the part of us that is not fully evolved. We incinerate the childish demand for instant gratification, using our hungers as fuel instead. This is tapas: burning out what no longer serves to create a burning enthusiasm for living, loving, and learning. We use intentional, kind discipline to tend to the fire in our ever-evolving inner hearts.

## Get Back in Your Box

I was watching the snowfall from the back of an Uber, zig-zagging through the Manhattan streets, wetly smooshed up against my wool-and-down bundled friends. Three colleagues and I spilled out onto the slushy curb in front of ABC Carpet and Home, a pricey, prestigious home decorating and design shop. Deepak Homebase, nestled into the gorgeous store's lofty upper regions, was hosting this elite event and the place was vibrating with excitement. Plus, even in the biting cold of February, the pulsing rhythm of New York City captivates me. The art, the innovation, and the aliveness of the metro vibe just resonates. In our stylish, urbanite boots, we strode into the lush event space, with photographers crouching, cameras flashing, faces turning to see and be seen.

Dr. Brené Brown was facilitating the gathering for the Nobel Women's Initiative, to honor and hear stories from a few of the women who had won the Nobel Peace Prize. I was thrilled to be in a room sparkling with powerful female changemakers, truly women to admire.

These women's stories, their battles, are not easy or glamorous. Many of them regularly risk their lives or their personal safety to catalyze change in the world. They are on the front lines, courageous and outrageous, true disruptors of political and societal ignorance. One of the Nobel laureates, Jody Williams, spoke about her work to ban landmines. She was surprisingly gritty, foul-mouthed, and real. I liked her immediately. She dispassionately spoke about her experienced trauma while working for peace in war-torn countries. She was a hands-on revolutionary, and her fearlessness was disarming, even slightly concerning. She was inspiring in a reckless way, and I was moved by her courage and determination.

I loved every minute of this occasion and alternated between being enthusiastically intimidated and feeling right at home. The prizewinners were bright, intelligent, powerful women. Of course, I wanted to hug everyone, connect with everyone, interact with everyone, and join everyone's cause. I had recently met a number of people from the legendary Fetzer Institute who were also in attendance. I felt aligned with the people around me and fully present from within. It was an expansive, soul satisfying experience, to know there are many others out there on the cutting edge, making waves to help the world evolve.

A few days after returning from this northeastern jaunt, I was on the phone with my ninety-three-year-old mother, relating my experience and sharing my excitement. I was bubbling over with stories and anecdotes about these modern-day heroines who were truly changing the world. I was describing how impactful their lives were, how they made me want to dig deeper and do more myself. I shared their successes and their failures, their heartbreak, and their joy. My mom listened quietly and as I concluded; the phone was disconcertingly silent. I took a few deep breaths in the elongated pause and waited for my mother's response.

She said, "Well, wasn't that a once in a lifetime experience for you. Now you just need to get back into your work in Atlanta, go back to teaching your weekly classes, and get on with things."

I took a few deep breaths, digesting her input, feeling its impact. I was so eager to share my fervor, I forgot who I was talking to; I opened myself to someone who is unaccustomed to uplifting other women's light. I felt as if my mother had said to get back in my box, to behave in the diminished way she thinks I should, to not shine my light too bright. I felt the familiar constriction low in my belly. But luckily, I have done this dance with her before.

My mom is a staunch Catholic and clutches a dogmatic belief system in her flecked, arthritic hands like a well-worn band of rosary beads. Once, at twenty-five years old, I had telephoned her to share that I was in love. Having just earned my BFA, my boyfriend and I had decided to move into a downtown artist loft together. I wasn't asking for her benediction exactly, but I was jittery about telling her, aware of her straight and narrow religious beliefs.

She had already met Tomás and liked him a lot. He was affable, talented, and at ease with himself. He and I were having a ball: making art, learning to scuba dive, and just being together, exploring the odd urban wasteland of downtown

THE FIRETENDER OF THE HEART · 163

Atlanta in the 1980s. As I shared our plans to cohabitate, I heard a gasp, then a strangled cry from her end of the phone, followed immediately by a full-fledged slam. She had hung up on me—and this was back in the day when you really could pound a receiver down into its clunky, receptive cradle.

Mom was an expert at stonewalling—using the silent treatment to either ice you out, punish you, or get her way. Previously, this tactic had worked on me. She would silently seethe with disdain and disapproval, slut-shaming me to the core. I was an adult; I was not a practicing Catholic and I knew what I wanted. It was difficult for her to understand that my spiritual beliefs were not the same as hers. I was tremulously claiming myself as a yogi, and it was time for me to stand independently. After a few failed attempts at connection and conversation, I let go. I felt the friction, the tapas, of not fixing it for once. Her style was to never talk about it again and act as if it wasn't happening. It took a while for us to reconnect, but I waited it out. I wasn't giving this one up just to please her.

The phone call about the Nobel Women's Initiative had an alarmingly similar tone. As her contractive comment landed fully, I took deep breaths and let myself feel her censure. Historically, I might have shut down, changed the subject, or ended the conversation, feeling the barb and wrapping myself around the fresh wound. However, if I am present and powerful, I can choose my response and heal the wound in the moment of its infliction. I settled my awareness in the center of my chest, in my inner heart, where the fire of transformation burns. I allowed the warmth of love to permeate, to spread through me. I poured love toward me, toward her, toward us, toward the moment. Filled with the genuine experience of many years of practice, I turned toward her, opened my heart, and simply said, "Mom, I'm just getting started."

### And Shine Like the Sun

Not everyone will celebrate our expansion as we grow and change. Not everyone knows how. Choosing evolution, joy, and self-confidence is not always supported by those around us. We begin to change, and change makes people uncomfortable. It is supposed to. That's why it takes courage.

Our loved ones might fear that we will grow away from them. And we might. We cannot control or dictate the trajectory of our growth. That's why it's scary—to us and to them. Spiritual growth, the actual growth of our spirit, takes us into the unknown territory of soul evolution. The yogis call this the experience of the *atman*, the essential essence of the self. When we trust ourselves enough to grow, especially when those around us would unknowingly try to limit us, we take a risk. We risk disconnection and shaming. But a deeper depth, a riskier risk, exists. It's the risk of not being an ally to our own soul. There is nothing more crushing, no act more debilitating than betraying yourself on a soul level.

*There is nothing more crushing,*
*no act more debilitating than betraying yourself*
*on a soul level.*

In the evolutionary process of real personal growth, we may become less familiar to our family. We are the ones changing the rules; we are stepping out of the familial, because what we have been doing is no longer working, and we recognize that. Then we dare to admit it, out loud, to other people! But outside our tight circle of comfort is our growth zone. Here, we can invite in a chosen family, a community of people who like us, understand us, and support our evolution. If our close people are concerned about our growth, we can be open and explain our process with them to create a shared experience. This allows us to connect and, hopefully, defuse their fear—and ours. Our growth zone holds the intriguing space of creativity and self-expression, and we long to explore that space and live there. Yes, we may become less constricted, less limited, less depressed, less *less*. This is why we are doing the work: to heal the less, and lean into... not just the more, but the more authentic.

## MINI PRACTICE

### BURN TO ASH

Fire—in Sanskrit, *agni*—is a universal agent of change honored by all wisdom traditions as a symbol of light and transformation. By transforming wood, wick, and wax into smoke and ash, the fire element reminds us that we too can transform, burning away what no longer serves us. This ritual can be done with a roaring outdoor campfire, a sacred *puja*—moving prayer—ceremony, or simply a lit candle.

*Technique*
Bring to mind what you would like to transform. Either write it on paper to burn in your fire, infuse it into a few grains of rice to make a puja offering, or hold it in your mind to offer into the candle flame. You may want to offer one or many things. Then, create your own ritual around it. Be creative and trust your intention. Your goal is a moment of true release, relinquishing your suffering into the fire, burning it to ash.

# This Bathroom Is Going to Kill Us

"This bathroom is going to kill us," Brandon huffed as he emerged, coughing and fuming through a billowing cloud of sheetrock dust. His dark jeans were smudged with stark streaks of spackle, his toolbelt was clanking, and he gripped a putty knife solidly in one hand.

He took in a disgruntled breath and waved dust from in front of his smeared, contorted face. He paused as grit rained noisily down behind him from the unfinished bathroom ceiling. He was having a meltdown, days in the making. He inhaled deeply and launched into a dramatic, full-throttle, spectacular temper tantrum. And he launched it fully onto me.

"This sink isn't even *supposed* to be centered. I don't care if the pipes look wrong—they bend, for God's sake."

My house was under construction, and I had hired Brandon, a longtime friend and student, to do the renovation. He was one of the original attendees of my AIDS and HIV+ Classes and was a creative, talented craftsman. He and I had met twenty years before in the Infectious Diseases Clinic of Grady Hospital where I was teaching. Like two long-lost friends who were just meeting for the first time, we ran across the room at each other, embraced, clicked spontaneously, and held on for dear life. Our valued friendship had weathered many storms, but we were enmeshed in a cantankerous conflict, and I was trying, really trying, to practice what I preach.

His thick, lush eyelashes flashed up and down, gray eyes daggering his scornful disdain. Suddenly he believed everyone was cheating him, nothing was clearly agreed upon, and he was furious at my one-hundred-year-old house. That marble tile, this ludicrous floating sink—these were all the obvious problem. It didn't have anything to do with him. He was flouncing his anguish around the room, threatening to bail out mid-project and leave in a glorious huff.

Brandon was constantly on the move, and even when he drove me crazy, I adored him. Like a gorgeous, gay butterfly, Brandon would vanish for months on end, flitting off to the next person, the next project, or the next town, always keeping it light. Over the years, he and I had bonded over so many things together: we walked mutual friends through death's door, survived epic green-juice-and-water fasts, laid encircled in crystals on a dark temple floor. We were into the various healing arts, willing to try anything to combat the terror of a diagnosis for our ever-expanding circle of young men with AIDS. So, we practiced yoga, meditation, and white tantric eye gazing. We belly-breathed our way into ecstatic giggle fits. We did twenty-four-hour chants in a tiny, sweltering outdoor shrine. We experienced ritual fire ceremonies, throwing handfuls of karmic chaff into the flames. We did sleepy sunrise meditations, trusted in Tibetan healing rites, and sat for sacred *yantra* paintings enacted by holy gurus. We walked through every version of health-inducing kumbaya we could find, so surely we could find our way to loving each other through the renovation of my bathroom.

"Calm down," I advised, which has never calmed anyone down, ever. "Let's take a break, go outside, and get some air."

I was pretty sure he was in over his head, pushing the edge of his skill set, possibly hovering out over the precipice of I-might-screw-this-up. I kept pausing and breathing through his escalating fireworks, practicing the art of non-reaction. I have been in many stressful throwdowns with people shooting arrows before. My best tools are quieter, but stealthily effective; not reacting, holding space, and bearing witness with someone else's pain should never be underestimated.

*Not reacting, holding space, and bearing witness with someone else's pain should never be underestimated.*

## Don't Take the Bait

At the root of non-reaction, we stand in depth and integrity and simply, patiently, frustratingly, follow one rule: don't take the bait. Just don't do it. Don't take it, even though it's extraordinarily tempting.

They are shooting barbs: aiming below the belt, throwing accusations, not playing fair. They are spoiling for a fight and trying to draw you into it, but don't take the bait. To accomplish this, you have to know you are under attack. The first red flag is the pain that comes when the initial barb strikes its intended target. Feel it. Breathe into it. Then listen as much as you talk. Don't react to the drama, the sucker punches, and the unfounded accusations. Most importantly, listen deeper than the everyday things—the paint color, the faucets, the money—to what need, what fear, or what unworthiness is arising.

*It's like subterranean listening, hearing what is being said while also attuning yourself to the emotion underneath it.*

It's like subterranean listening, hearing what is being said while also attuning yourself to the emotion underneath it. Remember, whatever that emotion is, it only comes up to be healed. That's why our old traumas resurface—they still have something to teach us.

As the pyrotechnics subsided, we sat outside in the dappled sunlight on my back deck and connected. We went through various conflict resolution practices, settling on the phrase, "I refuse to be enemies with you," which puts us on the same side of the table, looking at the problem together, instead of looking at each other as the problem. This insightful tool helps us focus on what our suffering is teaching us, instead of polarizing each other. "I refuse to be enemies with you" helps us feel the hurt more acutely and identify our emotions in the safe container of having no enemy.

We went further, using the compassion tool, "It only comes up to be healed." Whenever an old trauma pattern arises, it immediately gets our attention because it hurts so much. When we become aware of it, we use it to kindle tapas, the fire of transformation. My home renovation project had unearthed something for Brandon, and as we both sat and listened for what that something was, Brandon visibly calmed. We softened and grinned shyly at each other. In this, we held the friendship as more important than the renovation, which it was. After a few minutes, we turned the conversation to the aspect of the project that kept being mysteriously avoided. We discovered that there was a complex, intimidating challenge that was creating undue stress. After a bit, we also realized he had a trusted carpenter friend he could confer with and potentially engage to assist with the more daunting aspects of the job.

After further connection and reflection, Brandon's eyes welled over with tears. He broke open. He spoke of his relationship with his dad, his "not-enoughness," and his fear of inadequacy. I could see the pain begin to dissolve and resolve within him as he spoke. A few moments later, he chortled and claimed himself as a work in progress like the rest of us. I did too. We talked. We cared for each other. We figured it out. Then we hugged like we did in our first moment of meeting one another, holding onto each other, trusting in our ever-evolving experiences of life.

## The Fire of Becoming

The yogic practice of *tapas* is the practice of self-discipline, literally doing—or not-doing—something to generate friction. When we practice non-reaction and deprive the ego, we create the hot-throb space of restraint, of not-doing. As ayurvedic expert and author, Dr. John Douillard says, *"We want to be doing nothing but accomplishing everything. That's real power."* Non-reaction is intense, and we typically think of intensity as doing, but in not-doing you encounter a more difficult, more empowering option. You use discipline to avoid lashing out and create the space for your own transformation to occur.

> *Tapas burns. It burns the sticky emotional substance that keeps you stilted or bound to past patterns.*

Tapas burns. It burns the sticky emotional substance that keeps you stilted or bound to past patterns. Tapas means discipline, but if we look a little deeper, tapas is actually about discipline entwined with love.

Like many people, yogis can push ourselves in ways that are problematic. When willpower overtakes kindness, we have lost our way. We have become too driven, too tight, or too rigid. Our inner heart must be included in tapas, for tapas is intended to burn away anything that blocks the expression of love. Tapas creates compassionate discipline, but discipline nonetheless. A yogi's relationship with fire—the inner fire—is ongoing. We curate a relationship with transformation by burning out limitations, kindling a burning enthusiasm for life, and illuminating the brightest version of who we are.

We strive to burn everything that isn't the truest expression of us, everything that doesn't evolve us. We burn all this in the fire of our own awareness. Tapas instructs us to use suffering as fuel—and some of us are given rocket fuel—so stand back and think how far a rocket can fly.

## DEEP PRACTICE

### FANNING THE FIRE

Sometimes we want to pour gasoline on the fire of our own transformation. You know, throw the match, get inspired, get awake already. This technique, *bhastrika*, is a fire starter, named after the old-fashioned, triangular bellows used to fan flames into life. Here, the body is used like a bellows, powerfully pumping air in and out of the lungs. This fiery technique ignites vibrant emotional metabolism, so we can thoroughly embrace and digest the chaos of the world and our reactions to the world. This is a big ask, because we react, a lot. We all have plenty of fuel to burn—virtual woodpile stacks of heartbreak, resentment, judgment, and opinion. All are fuel for growth.

This breath method enhances the growth process

by fanning the natural fire in the body, increasing the heat of transformation so we can skillfully navigate the intense experiences of life. Use this practice when attempting to intentionally change a behavior by holding open space—like when you have been hurt and feel angry but want to burn the anger instead of burning the one who made you angry. So, instead of burning down relationships, we consume life with mindful, compassionate presence.

*Bhastrika Breath Technique*
Do this breath sitting or lying down, not standing or driving! Inhale fully through the nose, expanding the lungs, ribcage, belly, and abdomen. Exhale through the nose, powerfully contracting the navel toward the spine. Continue with strong inhalations and exhalations, really pumping the belly bellows. Keep a steady, moderate pace. The breath is full, complete, and powerful. Start with thirty to sixty seconds and work up to three to four minutes.

To end, inhale and retain the breath for a few seconds, calmly circulating prana, or energy, throughout the body. Exhale and hold the breath out for fifteen to sixty seconds. Deep sensations can occur as you retain the exhalation. Holding the breath out, explore your emotional body by feeling, observing, and noticing what you feel. Release anything angry, tight, blocked, or irritated. Welcome any and all sensations. Feel whatever you feel. Let it gently resolve itself as you relax. Then take a few deep, clearing breaths. Do one to three rounds.

# 8
# THE EYE OF THE STORM

**Santosha:** (sahn-TOW-shuh) contentment, equanimity, being at ease

*"People take different roads seeking fulfillment and happiness. Just because they are not on your road, does not mean they are lost."*

THE DALAI LAMA

## He's Having One Over on Me

*I have just been lied to, robbed and made a total fool. He's having one over on me. He's using again,* I thought to myself.

Standing in a cloud of exhaust as my sweet, funny, tragic brother accelerated his overpacked Jeep out of the parking lot, I felt the spicy hot chilies stinging my tongue from our shared Thai meal. I stood, transfixed, but unaware it would be our final meal for years. He was running. He was lying. I could feel it, but kept pushing it away, unable to acknowledge the stomach-clenching ambiguity. I sensed the deceit but couldn't fully accept it because I really didn't want it to be true. He was such a good liar, the unapplauded skill of many an alcoholic.

Pete started drinking at thirteen, shooting heroin a year later. I was nine, then ten, then a hundred and twenty-two. In his own words, addiction took hold of him at the first sip, like a fireball of intensity, a raging brain fever that never lost its grip. After that lunch, which in hindsight was spackled with a thick swath of expertly applied bullshit, Pete disappeared into the alleyways and streets of San Francisco for a full decade.

Watching my favorite brother struggle through cycles of heroin addiction, alcoholism, and homelessness taught me to worry in a very specific way. I was always ready for catastrophe to strike. It was like a background noise I could not quite mute, an underground fissure that could give way in an instant, but mostly I remembered to walk over the cracks, maintaining precarious, hard-won balance. There were treatments centers, years of supposed sobriety, times I was certain he was clean. There were vodka bottles, handguns and needles littered across scarred coffee tables. There were dreams of homeownership with imagined backyards and unmet rescue dogs named Riley. There was an indelible undercurrent of uncertainty that just never left—until he did.

My oldest sister is a neonatal nurse, who tends the sickest babies daily. She got the call and called me: dead of kidney failure. After a lifetime of heroin, vodka, and cheap, greasy cheeseburgers, Pete was found collapsed on the Atlanta streets, just a few miles from my home. As my sisters and I were scrambling to claim his body, some family member suggested we just leave him in the city morgue. I thought, *"Over my dead body. I couldn't take care of him in life. I'll be damned if I don't take care of him in death."* I felt he died nearby because he knew we would find him, my sisters and I, even if he couldn't devour enough of his shame to just come home.

Weary, heartbroken, broken open, the three of us walked into the funeral home to claim his cold, pale body and to hold him one last time. Emaciated and gaunt, he did and did not look like himself, in the way dead people often do.

Ritual around death holds great meaning for me, so my sisters and I began the death rites my guru had shared. We cleaned him head-to-toe, loving him with every swipe of the cloth, touching the hallowed ground of every crevice, so much abused, so nakedly unadorned. Bathing him with rosewater, rubbing his scarred, tattered skin with warm, fragrant oil. Pete did not survive the calamity of our upbringing, but the three sisters, all warrior women, held him in death like the beloved child he mostly never was and that we, all of us, never quite were. We wrapped him in shawls with holy mantras woven into the cloth, sacred words to safeguard him in death. We draped him with garlands, anointed him with shared memories, and adorned him with flower petals. We loved him, laughed with him, sang to him, said goodbye to him. We poured everything we could into him and then we let him go.

All of these expressions of love would ride with Pete into the impersonal oven that would incinerate his tired, beloved form. The ash of his body was returned to us in a thick plastic bag, heavier and lighter than you would ever suspect. The ash of the dead is potent with all the pain, all the passion, all the purpose of a lifetime. We reverently placed his ash in a beautiful, polished wooden box, and I could feel him sarcastically rolling his big, green eyes as we drove him to the river.

## Balancing on Thin, Thick Air

Seeking to regain my equanimity without my brother in the world instigated a bone-deep rebalancing. I felt the ground beneath me, the earth spinning slowly, imperceptibly different with the weight of his presence gone, his contrapposto to mine, his absence already absolute. Mourning. My lifelong mantra—that cadence of perpetual concern and unease—went missing. Living in uncertainty had become an aptitude, a coping, a constantly refined skill. When would I hear from him again? Where was he? When would the phone call come?

It has come, beloved. It is done. Close the door. Open the heart. It has come.

Handful after handful, we released his ashes into the icy river, windy gusts blowing it back, coating each of us with bleak gray dust. Like a final caress, a spirit touch, ash upon skin, upon clothes, upon tear-streaked faces. We plunged our bare hands into the remnants of Peter, throwing him, hurling him, releasing him softly into the water and into the wind.

## The Eye of the Storm

When Pete was in active addiction, his chaos would crash-land into my life, abrupt and intense. It would lift me by the throat and pin me into equanimity. Holding myself at the eye of this storm, I learned to open into the moment and connect to the sensations in my body: the panic and the breathlessness I felt while witnessing his turmoil. To embody contentment when my heart was good and truly broken was to split myself open to being fully alive, trusting in the brutal, beautiful processes of life.

*To embody contentment when my heart was good*
*and truly broken was to split myself open to*
*being fully alive, trusting in the brutal,*
*beautiful processes of life.*

I was learning to use all of life as fuel and grieve losses in real time. The yogis call this *santosha*, or contentment, living as the eye of the storm. It's being okay with the intensity and wildness of all of it. Whether we're going through a storm of stress, betrayal, or even death, when we expand through our experiences instead of contracting away from them, we inhabit an ability to just... be okay. We learn to live in harmony inside any emotion, be it outrage, boredom, heartbreak, or loneliness. We tolerate and open, lean in and become. We learn real courage, and in so doing, we love our way through all of it.

We feel deeply when we embody santosha because we are content with who and how we are. It's embodied acceptance, and it refines our emotional metabolism. This creates powerful engagement, where we consume the whole of experience. In life, we have to consume the world lest it consume us. We instigate the ability to tolerate and digest the pain and chaos of the world around us. None of us do this perfectly. We all collapse under the tempest sometimes, like I did upon my brother's death. If we cannot face and accept the suffering, we suffer more, because we are either pushing it away in denial, clinging to it in sorrow, or compensating for it by overcompensating.

*Santosha asks us*
*to change our relationship with our suffering.*

Santosha asks us to change our relationship with our suffering: to develop empathy and understanding for our own woundedness, our most shameful pain, to soften, open, and allow our hardest moments to evolve us, and to love anyway.

### Put Your Yoga Where Your Mouth Is

In the *Bhagavad Gita*, one of the pillars of yoga is described as *karma yoga*, which means the yoga of action. This concept teaches us to learn the life-affirming tools of yoga and then put them to good use in the world. Karma yoga asks us to put our yoga where our mouth is: to want wholeness, equanimity, and contentment for all people, not just for ourselves.

My brother Peter inspired my creation of a karma yoga street relief program that I started in Atlanta. Between his homelessness and my guru's advice to "feed everyone, love everyone, serve everyone," Street Meals has fed tens of thousands of meals to people experiencing homelessness and marginalization. Peter laughed when I told him about this, during one of his longer periods of sobriety.

"One of the best things about twelve step meetings is the food," Pete shared. "The coffee usually sucks, but there's always a box of doughnuts or a plate of homemade brownies in the back somewhere." Pete loved food; he loved to eat and ate almost anything with gusto. He was fun to feed because his love of food was exuberant and genuine. The day we had this conversation, we had gathered at my sister's little stone house, surrounded by lush gardens, celebrating her birthday. I felt content to be with them: sister, brother, and sister. I was content to simply be together, to share our family bond.

Shoving a fat, domed, freshly baked cupcake into his very large mouth, Peter started laughing, sputtering crumbs across the linen tablecloth. "Life is pretty good," he said, happily, gathering crumbs.

We ride the wind, navigating life's inevitable storms and gusts. It is all good, even when it's hard. It's still full of possibility. Ultimately, life is good because it all evolves us, and in that knowledge, we can truly find contentment.

## Santosha: The Dirty Word—Contentment

The Sanskrit word *santosha* is defined as equanimity, peace, well-being, and evenness, but also as contentment. My guru, Ma Jaya, used to say that she didn't like this niyama, because to her it suggested laziness. Contentment can breed stagnation. But in yoga, the meditations, practices, breaths, ethics, and ideals are neutral. They are healing and effective. They might provoke a reaction. They might kindle kundalini. They could ignite a process of transformation, spin us on our heads, or irritate us to our core. They might, in Ma's eloquent words, make us feel like a rock in the washing machine, banging into all the other rocks, which are the other people in our life. The idea is to come out of the rock tumbler smooth and at peace with the other rocks—content.

Ma would explain that if we are too content, we can be unwilling to look at our flaws or unable to do the knotty work of our own evolution. Yet connecting to innate well-being is a form of yoga. We can be doing a yoga pose, wrangling kid's schedules, or disagreeing with a colleague, but if we take one deep breath, we are right there, in equanimity, where it's all good.

Santosha creates a quality of practiced acceptance. In challenging situations and jubilant ones, we feel our feelings and open to them, accepting the situation and our reaction to it. We stop judging so much and start trusting that everything we experience is teaching us, and that we have the power of individual choice. Unconditional acceptance does not mean we accept injustice or unethical treatment. It means we see it for what it is and choose mindfully how to respond.

## Not Meditating on a Mountaintop

But how do you address difficult, impactful occurrences like addiction, manipulation, infidelity, racism, violence, or corruption? How are we supposed to be content with that?

The social justice of yoga would have us examine our own values and ethics. Are we treating people of other races as equals? Do we speak up from a place of kind curiosity when others in our circle say something homophobic? Do we hire or empower colleagues from different religions? Do we benefit from keeping others on the rung below us? These questions may stir up our unexamined biases, but that is real yoga: to not just stay content with how we are now, but to use the practices to evolve and grow.

As we learn equanimity, I should note that we are still human beings, still in the world, getting stirred up, getting entangled, getting hurt, and even getting angry or resentful. We see how santosha can help us navigate difficult questions, like ethical or moral issues, but can it help us maintain well-being through the absurd or mundane situations of life? For instance, can we maintain equilibrium in heavy traffic? When we lose our keys for the sixth time that day? When we are overly hungry? When no one else ever replaces the toilet paper roll?

Ancient yogis meditating on a mountaintop is one thing, but here we are trying to pay the rent, be in love, and extract the joy out of a complex modern life. If we are attempting to experience everyday equanimity, we have to bring santosha into the things we do each day.

Take, for example, your day-to-day yoga practice. If we are content with where we are, we stop trying to "perform" a yoga pose and enjoy the deep hip stretch, even if the pose looks imperfect. We accept our bodies as they are—tall or short, curvaceous or thin, flexible or stiff, any gender, race, or ability—even if society does or will not. We love our extra fat roll that is pooching out, obstructing our efforts into a pose. We remember that getting to be alive in a gorgeously distinct body is an extraordinary gift, instead of listing all the things wrong with us. We become kinder to ourselves, allowing space to be okay as we are.

Then, we take equanimity outside ourselves. We stop trying to demean, control, or change other people, even when their ignorance harms us. We navigate difficult conversations with compassion—conversations that include opposing views. We leave room for growth. We demonstrate and encourage it. We love people as they are, even when we do not love their beliefs, behaviors, or unconscious biases. We communicate our needs and hear theirs. We love ourselves with all our imperfections as we go out into the world and love others with all of theirs. We remember that well-being is a choice, as is growth, and we can choose it for ourselves.

### The Deeper Cut

Practicing yoga's many techniques can take us far from contentment. It can open up emotional pain and even reawaken trauma. Working with emotional pain or trauma differs from working with everyday mental chatter. It often provokes a bigger reaction, but each nugget of trauma we unpack reveals a hidden piece of our authenticity. When we get hurt, betrayed, or brutalized, we fragment. We break. We splinter into various pieces. Then the protective, unhealed substance of that trauma wraps itself around those fragments of our true self, holding that trueness tight in a clenched fist of old pain. If we can lovingly pry our fingers away from holding this wound so tightly, we can emancipate a fragment of our real selves.

However, it doesn't feel this way when we first touch that core of inner misery. We tend to flinch, draw back, or pull away. We lose our contentment because it hurts, and we have already been hurt in the initial wounding. We instinctively avoid revealing this sensitive space because we are afraid of being wounded again. When we can befriend our most intense experiences, we create space for our own healing. We cultivate santosha, a kind regard toward ourselves and toward the explosion of experience that may be revealed. Knowing the wound holds a key to our well-being can make us bolder about taking on the work.

## Lashing Out, Lashing In

The key to living as the eye of the storm and mastering contentment during conflict is awareness. It makes you strong enough to say "no" when "no" is the most conscious option—like when your brother starts using again and tries to con you in countless different ways. If we get activated by an interaction, as I often did with my brother, and if we have awareness that we are activated, we can make a conscious choice. It's okay to be angry about the situation, the bad choices, or the mistake. It's not okay to make the other person feel like a mistake. We also must not make ourselves feel like a mistake. It takes strength, compassion, and skill to hold clear boundaries that honor everyone involved. Contentment means you love peace, but it does not make you a doormat.

Let's say we choose not to lash out, blame, or offload our anger onto the other person. If we are not externalizing our pain, what happens to the volatile tide of internal emotion? Is it possible for us to be wise in a deluge of pain? If we do not lash out, how do we ensure we don't "lash in" and turn the blame inward? Lashing out is a form of blame, putting the source of the hurt and damage outside ourselves. Lashing in is a form of shame, putting the source of the hurt or damage inside. We make ourselves the problem, swallowing or internalizing the pain.

*When we lash in, we can convince ourselves*

*of our own unworthiness.*

When we lash in, we can convince ourselves of our own unworthiness. Blame and shame take us out of the wholeness of ourselves. We empower a mere fragment of ourselves to call the shots. Santosha asks us to see beyond these twin coping mechanisms and center ourselves as the eye of the storm. Here we embody the quiet stillness of just being. We remain balanced and steady. We keep our cool. We kindly and clearly choose how to respond.

Lashing up is not a good option either. Yelling at God, your sacred source, or the universe is just not that rewarding.

It creates sacred disconnection instead of the union of spirit that yoga hopes to instill. The yogic idea is that life is like school—we are here to learn. Understanding how to be content while we do the work creates trust and makes all of it a little more joyful.

## MINI PRACTICE

### RADICAL ACCEPTANCE

When we stop lashing out, in or up, we are on the precipice of radical acceptance. Acceptance is different than capitulation because genuine acceptance heals us. If we accept ourselves completely, we are totally okay with who and how we are in any given moment. This is a practice of equanimity. What if you could accept everything about yourself, as you are today?

*Technique*
Sit for meditation, spine long, eyes closed. Take a few deep breaths, in and out. Set an intention to open to radical acceptance and to explore the sensations this evokes.

Accept:
- Every mistake you have ever made.
- Every mark on your body.
- Every success you have ever had.
- Every moment of joy.
- Every experience of pain you have ever felt.
- Every desire, every moment of lust or longing.

- Every experience of disconnection.
- Every moment of love.
- Everything you are experiencing now.

Accept it all, the way you accept nature, the way you accept a sunrise, the feeling of the wind, or the falling of snow. Be present and feel, not judging, just allowing.

- Take a few deep breaths. Settle into your body, being aware of how all these statements feel to you today. Offer yourself embodied acceptance, accepting everything about yourself.
- Release judgment so you can be open and simple, breathing acceptance in and out using long deep breaths.
- Feel acceptance until it feels natural and alive in you, like a sensation of just being okay with all of it, just being at peace.
- Accept that at this moment, you are exactly as you're meant to be.

## Which Way Is Up

My back was killing me. My sacrum seemed to be facing left while my legs were facing right, and no matter how many yoga postures I did, I could not find any relief. I experimented with gentle yoga twists; nothing changed. I bowed deeply forward, stretching and elongating; still suffering. I cautiously bowed backward; I yelped in pain and started to cry. I rested in Child's Pose, but nothing was relieving my lower back distress. It was excruciating. I couldn't sit down without a piercing agony shooting across my low back. Breath by breath, I was losing my equanimity because nothing can make you cranky like ongoing physical pain.

Yogis, like everyone else, sometimes wrench their bodies and need help getting back into proper alignment. I decided to visit the chiropractor. Dr. Bob Dalton works his healing magic in an unusual, eclectic style. Instead of a private appointment, he has five treatment tables set in a loose circle in a medium-sized, dimly lit room. I tentatively slid onto the last open table, measuring out every careful, painful move. Native American flute music wafted through the cozy space. Dr. Bob worked on one patient for a few minutes, then moved smoothly to the next, adjusting as he went, allowing time for each adjustment to settle as he worked his way around the circle. Sometimes people would chat back and forth between tables, but mostly it was quiet—a calm, contemplative space.

My back misalignment was jammed—super jammed. Bob couldn't get it to budge. A triangular inversion device was tucked into an alcove in a dark, solitary corner of the room. Bob had never used this device with me before, but I was familiar with inversions. I love doing headstands and practice them regularly. I was willing to try almost anything to get out of this intense pain, which was stealing my santosha, my cup-half-full sense of well-being.

Bob instructed me on how to use the inversion apparatus, bear-hugging me into it. The device hooked my legs securely behind my knees. Together, we slowly tipped me forward, flipping me topsy-turvy, hanging from my legs with my feet in the air, like a bat clinging to the roof of a dark cave, the top of my head hovering just off the floor. I dangled over the earth, swaying softly, clutching the sides of the apparatus, hoping for some relief. Still in excruciating pain, I cautiously released my hands off the cool silver bars of the machine, extending them over my head, touching the textured carpet with my fingertips. I took a deep breath, inhaling the lingering remnant of Bob's brief, healing embrace, the earthy aroma of sandalwood mingling with the frosty zing of breath mint.

Suddenly, I felt a lurch: a distinct bone-crunching pop deep in my lower back. I shuddered in a full-body quiver.

Like a freight train, energy flashed up my spine, intense, powerful, and wild. It unleashed a rush of vitality, which I couldn't contain. I started to laugh, and hilarity enveloped me, thundering out of my mouth. I was caught in a torrent of unexpected, unstoppable laughter. In this quiet, respectful healing sanctuary, I was roaring—an outrageous, full belly laugh that rolled across the room, banging into the peaceful space. It was like joy itself had launched up my upside-down spine.

My ears filled with whooshing. My body filled with tingling. My spine was vibrating with electrified wildness. I laughed harder than I ever have, before or since, howling in astonished delight. It was like laughing in church, when you know you shouldn't, but you just can't stop. Tears sprang from my eyes, obscuring my vision, pooling into my ears, then spilling in full, lush streams. Guffawing. Screeching. Bellowing.

Laughter filled up the space, became its own healing, bouncing off ceilings, ricocheting off walls. I laughed with total surrender, fully out loud, for a solid couple of minutes, glee pouring out from the depths of my very being. It was like misery unlocked its gate and joy gushed forth in a deluge.

Wiping my face clear as the laughter subsided, I could see and hear what was happening in the room. From my upside-down perch, I saw Bob's slim form, draped over another patient, both of them wailing with delight. The entire room was in an uproar of elation, raucous laughter spreading across us all. I was off again, all of us were, another tangent cascading over us.

Every time they tried to ask me what set me off, the laughter would spill over again, surging out. There was no explaining. No logic. No mind. I finally sputtered out the word *kundalini* and we all dissolved into hysterics again. We laughed until we laughed ourselves dry.

I did not maintain composure. I leaned into pure joy and rode it for all it was worth. I have done the same with rage or sorrow, allowing it to pour through me, with full access to all of my senses. Equanimity was somewhere off in the distance. My best way back to it was through the full expression of feeling.

Healing can happen when a sensation or experience arises from the inner depths, be it sorrow or unprecedented joy. Healing happens when something that has been knotted or hidden is opened and released. The rising of kundalini—that mystical energy that beckons us awake—can unblock things, like a storehouse of happiness, secretly shoved into the basement of our spines.

I was effervescent, lit up head to toe. My back felt fine, amazing even. I didn't have words for any of it, but that joy lasted for hours, days, even weeks. Kundalini, the energy of awareness, rose. Laughter was its own language of joy.

*Santosha aligns us with inner presence.*

## Joy Is the Raw Material

Santosha aligns us with inner presence. It establishes an ongoing sense of well-being that guides us through the storms of life. We ride the waves of existence, not clinging, not avoiding, just being present and practicing deep witnessing.

We sometimes think we are supposed to live in the middle ground of peaceful acceptance all the time. The truth is sometimes life is intense. Equanimity is not about limiting the force of our emotions or experiences. It is holding our center even when there is great feeling, whether its love or pain. When I allow myself this full range of experience, I become more fully alive. I understand I am not my rage. I am not my joy. I allow these occurrences to pour through me and reveal to me who I am beyond them.

One quality at the core of equanimity is gratitude. Gratitude is a powerful human emotion. It's a way of focusing on the good things in life. When we are thankful for all experience, not just the positive ones, we remember that we get to live all the wildness of life. Not we *have to*, we *get to*. We remember to say thank you for everything life hands us, which makes us happier. Plus, "Positive psychology and mental health researchers in the past few decades have established an overwhelming connection between gratitude and good health. Keeping a gratitude journal causes less stress, improves the quality of sleep, and builds emotional awareness" (Seligman, Steen, Park, & Peterson, 2005). While writing a gratitude list privately in a journal is effective, speaking your thanks aloud to the people you appreciate can be even more powerful. Gratitude is the raw material for joy. Joy is the raw material for contentment.

# DEEP PRACTICE

## THE EYE OF THE STORM

Deep breathing is a prelude to embodied peace. It works with the nervous system, housed inside our spine in the deepest physical recesses of our being. When we breathe correctly, we calm our nervous system and the fight, flight, or freeze response. We reset the amygdala, the primitive part of our brain that is habitually reactive. To live as the eye of the storm, mastery over this primal brain response is imperative, and we get there fastest through mastery over the breath.

The yoga practice of *pratyahara*, the purposeful withdrawal of the senses, tells us to draw into the center of our being. To be in the eye of the storm, we must deepen our inner resolve and build strength, tenacity, and resilience. Our goal is to draw our senses into ourselves and be outwardly present at the same time. The world can be a jangling place. Being the eye of the storm is not an escape from that; it's a living, intentional response to it. We stand in the eye of the storm when life is raging and embody authentic power—not *power over*, but *power to*.

In this practice, we draw our senses into the *sushumna*—translated as "grace-filled"—the central energy column along the spine. The sushumna is a place of refuge, a place to reconnect to our inner resources. Breathing through the core of the body, we establish a calm center where we can stand as the eye of the storm one breath at a time.

*The Eye of the Storm Breath Technique*

- Sit for meditation or do this on the go, whenever or wherever you need it. Take very long, deep breaths.
- Throughout this practice use the Ujjayi sound you learned in Chapter One: The Breath That Changes Everything. It's the sound of the wind, the "hhhhh" sound of the breath that escorts you back into the moment.
- Begin an Eye of the Storm Breath by inhaling up the spine from the tailbone to the top of the head. Of course, the physical breath is going in and out of your lungs, but here you work with prana, the life force, directing energy up and down the spine.
- Then exhale from the top of the head back down to the base of the spine, directing prana down.
- Continue up the spine as you inhale, down as you exhale for ten to thirty minutes, riding the inbreath to the top of the head and the outbreath to the bottom of the spine.
- Draw your awareness deeper and deeper within, establishing equanimity with yourself as the eye of storm, riding the current of breath up and down the central column.

# 9
# THE SPACE BETWEEN THE THOUGHTS

**Svadhyaya:** (svahd-YAI-yuh) self-study,
introspection, contemplation

*"Quiet the mind and the soul will speak."*

MA JAYA

## Cavorting with the Monkeys of the Mind

For ten solid days, I awakened to the resonant, hollow chime of giant Tibetan bells reverberating across the mountains, summoning me to the chilly predawn meditation hall. Plopping down on a chubby zafu cushion next to purple sweat pants guy, I bound myself snug inside a thick wool shawl, spine erect. Placing my steaming mug of tea on the rough-hewn wood floor, I watched dust motes dancing through the shafts of early sunlight. Inhaling the fragrant, fleeting scent of burning incense, I closed my eyes and felt my breath. I dropped into the quiet and attempted to meditate for endless hours per day. In a rustic Buddhist sanctuary in the North Carolina mountains, the daily routine was simple: meditate a lot, eat breakfast in silence; meditate a lot more, eat lunch in silence; do a walking meditation outside and then meditate the afternoon away, watching patiently while my mind goes slowly insane.

I was in my twenties, enrolled in yet another silent meditation retreat, and weirdly enough at this young age, I loved it. Upon arriving at the remote refuge, I felt engulfed in spaciousness and silence. A lean, gray-haired monk greeted me, guided me through the registration process, then showed me around the pastoral grounds. From the first moment, I was instructed to immerse myself in the practice of intentional silence.

In yoga, this is a form of self-study called *svadyaya*, a method of observing yourself to winnow away what you are not, so you can be what you are. The Buddhists call this *vipassana*, or silent meditation retreat. The yogis call it *mauna*, intentional silence. Whatever you call it, these monks were serious about it: Please cast your eyes down when you encounter others. No whispering, giggling, talking, socializing, or connecting. Don't introduce yourself to your roommates. Do not meet or talk to any other retreat participants until the final day. We have a stick and—with your permission—we are not afraid to use it.

The intent is to use mindfulness tools to access our deeper nature, heal trauma, and address and ultimately tame the "monkeys of the mind." The second of *Patanjali's Yoga Sutra* states, *"Yoga chitta vritti nirodha,"* or yoga happens when the fluctuations of the mind cease. In other words, to achieve a state of union or wholeness, you have to calm the restless nature, or the monkeys, of the mind.

*Silent meditation is wildly effective*

*but excruciating in its own quiet way.*

Silent meditation is wildly effective but excruciating in its own quiet way. The only loud thing is the frenetic chaos of the restless, hungry, blaming, wounded, insatiable mind—those same darn monkeys. If yoga happens when the fluctuations of the mind cease, when the monkeys settle into stillness, I wanted to experience that moment, however fleeting or difficult to attain. My friend, colleague and author of *The Energy Codes*, Dr. Sue Morter, says "The mind is always trying to drive the bus. It's trying to do something that it isn't built to do. It's built to serve the soul."

So, to quiet my mind, I meditated. I meditated no matter how unruly my mind was, day after day, then vipassana retreat after vipassana retreat, I showed up and sat. I breathed and wept silently. I raged inaudibly in my own quietude. I sang noiseless songs, flowing between the ridiculously boppy Sesame Street theme song to Van Morrison, growling me "Into the Mystic." I repeated mantras to override the ceaseless songs. I sang silent songs to drown out the mantras. I relived childhood memories, unearthing prickly, encrusted treasures—not only the traumas but the delights such as running with chubby, brown child legs down Nantasket Beach, trailing seaweed tails, squealing in the sunlight and salt water.

I rescripted arguments, resentments, and rationales, justifying why I was right, why I should heroically win in every conflict. I thought up incredible art projects, then rejected them as inane. I imagined a career out of teaching yoga and cast that aside as pure fantasy. I thought. I looked for the space between the thoughts. I felt the feelings of a lifetime coalesce under a single breath, burbling up through the thick fugue of memory, and erupting to the surface of my awareness. I breathed the heartbreak in. I breathed it out again. I sat. I allowed. I befriended. I grieved. I began to heal. I attained calmness. I touched moments of genuine tranquility and inner peace only to feel the next roil of anguish begin its heavy, bestial trajectory upward.

*I touched moments of genuine tranquility and inner peace only to feel the next roil of anguish begin its heavy, bestial trajectory upward.*

### Where Is My Bubble?

I loved, basked in, resisted, and took refuge in ten days of silent introspection. The Buddhist prefects would pace slowly, methodically through the room, stick in hand, ready to gently whack a willing but wayward meditator back into the moment. When the closing day rolled around and the final lunch was served, I was so accustomed to the communal silence, to the protective cloak of anonymity, it was jarring to have the other participants begin to chat about daily, inconsequential things. People were talking, introducing themselves, doing what people do. I was so deep into the silence that I wasn't prepared to come back. How could everyone just start talking like this? I felt an internal friction at the sudden, jolting social demand. I thought we were all chilled-out monks here, merging with the mists of time. I don't want to talk about my job, my hometown, my relationship status. Wait, are you hitting on me? Where is my bubble?

I edged to the side of the room and sat at one of the unoccupied circular tables, set down my earthenware bowl, my fragrant, cinnamon-scented oatmeal untouched, raisins speckling its gooey, glossy surface. I took a deep breath and listened for my heart. I let myself open to the people here, to the gentle camaraderie unfolding all around me. I softened, taking my time in this transition back to regular interactions, to everyday living. Being in the silence was no longer difficult, but simply being human was. These were some of the first hints that I might have an inclination toward contemplative life. I might be a monk. Or a yoga monk. Or a yogi. The dichotomy of being in the world but not of it would call to me, teach me, rearrange me, and define me. A spiritual calling was calling out to me, but I wasn't sure what my answer was. Curious, I turned uncertainly, inquisitively back to the world.

Looking up as a fellow meditator gestured silently to sit next to me, I cleared my rusty throat, smiled, and softly said, "Welcome."

## Svadhyaya: The Space Between the Thoughts

The fourth niyama, svadhyaya, or self-study, says that to be our authentic, radiant selves, we have to practice. We must care for ourselves deeply, attune ourselves to our own innate rhythms, and learn how we most clearly resonate with life. We must practice embodying our own unique truth. We do this because happiness doesn't just happen—at least not in an ongoing, lived way. We have to apply ourselves to master it. Anything we want to excel at, we have to practice. I don't expect to pick up a violin and know how to play. I have to grasp the correct manner in which to hold the bow, learn finger and chin placement, and study the musical scales. I must attune myself to the instrument and understand how it sings. I need to dedicate myself to regular practice to play a harmonious song. I must also dedicate myself to regular self-study to live a radiant, harmonious life.

Svadhyaya teaches us to study our experience of being human in order to thrive. This cultivates a willingness to draw lessons from both our mistakes and our successes. Through the disciplines of non-reaction, equanimity, and conscious choice, we train our minds to remain in open curiosity. When we meditate or use mindfulness techniques—like the ones in this book—we develop skills to understand ourselves.

*When we breathe to deepen our awareness,*

*we get closer to our truth.*

When we breathe to deepen our awareness, we get closer to our truth. These self-observation tools inspire us to study the nature of our own minds, which is essential.

In Chapter 6.6, the *Bhagavad Gita* says, "For one who has conquered the mind, the mind is the best of friends; but for one who has failed to do so, the mind will remain the greatest enemy." Svadhyaya challenges us to train our minds to see between and beyond our thoughts. A common meditation credo is "You are not your thoughts." When we comprehend this, we glimpse the sky of the mind, with thoughts drifting through like clouds passing through the sky. We experience the spaciousness of the higher mind, that steady field of presence. Thoughts can lead us into all kinds of chaos, but the inner self remains behind those thoughts, waiting for us to look deeper and remember our essential self. We need tools to open up the space between the thoughts and lovingly move the thoughts to the side, so we can experience our own expansive nature.

# The Silence Calls Out to You

A silent meditation retreat is persistently uncomfortable for the first few days. When we shift from focusing outwardly on the life around us to focusing internally on contemplation, we are pulled through tiers of thought, opinion, and emotion. As we unshackle ourselves from the constant demands of the daily world, all the layers and fragments of experience begin to release, reconfigure, then coalesce in ever-deepening silence.

Nowadays, with so many of us excessively plugged in, intentionally going offline is empowering. We can choose to unplug from the cell phone, social media, email, text—all the input and the devices. A media fast may seem extreme, but it will help us tame the monkeys, calm the jumpy nature of the modern, media-influenced mind, and find our inner voices so we can hear who we are from the inside out.

Breaking the habit of chronic virtual connection allows space for real-time connection to the moment and the environment we are living in. Once we begin to deepen our relationship with sacred silence, unplugging elicits an enormous sensation of relief, an intentional casting off, an unburdening. Engaging in a deep, long unplug—like an extended retreat—can enable us to intentionally lay down the demands, both internal and external, and come back into a quiet relationship with simple being.

In this space, the silence calls out to you with its emptiness. You listen and respond. Healing becomes a phenomenon, a process to be experienced, an actuality. In the silence, understanding and allowing open you up over and over into being. Svadhyaya means you study being. You study being you until you just are. You just are you.

## PLEASE TAKE MY PHONE

Svadhyaya is all about getting quieter so you can
know yourself more fully. It's about clearing the field
of the mind so you can access a richer experience.
By addressing the constant, overwhelming bombard-
ment of information, this powerful practice dramatically reduces unnecessary external input. It creates an
opportunity to observe how that enormous volume
of content agitates the already restless nature of our
minds. It also creates a container—in the spirit of a
silent meditation retreat—to explore what happens
when you make an intentional healing choice by yourself and for yourself. Of course, you can enlist friends
and cohorts to join you, but the daily, moment-by-moment choice to refrain from media is still all yours.

*Media Fasting Technique*
Create a Media Fast for half, one, three, seven, or ten
days. Write your ideas of what this will contain. Sign
and date it, creating a contract with yourself. Place
this written agreement on your altar and read it each
morning when you sit for meditation.

**Media Fast: Personal Empowerment Pledge**
You can use this form or create your own.

*Intention:*
I, (print your name) _____ make a
commitment to give myself more time and space. I

commit to doing an intentional Media Fast to create a calm, clear mind and to instill well-being. I am choosing to do this because (list three or more reasons):

1. _____

2. _____

3. _____

*Plan:*

For (write a number) _____ days, I will intentionally refrain from (circle all that apply):

- Text
- Instagram
- Facebook
- Twitter
- TikTok
- Email
- News Feeds
- Google
- Television
- Streamed Shows
- Newspapers
- Magazines
- Podcasts
- Cell phone
- Tablet/Pad
- Gaming device
- E-Reader
- Smartwatch

*Daily Practice:*

- Read your intention aloud each morning to remember why you are choosing this practice.
- Sit for the following Awareness Meditation daily. Using your finger pads, count ten very long deep

breaths in and out, breathing in awareness and breathing out stress.

Then answer these questions:
How does media affect my self-worth?
During this Media Fast, do I have more time?
And if so, what am I choosing to do with it?
Am I more present? More connectable? Kinder?

Have fun, be creative, and explore the practice.

*Signature:*

I, (sign your name) _____ promise to do my best and be kind myself through the process. I promise to choose a length of time that feels doable and that supports my efforts.

*Date:* _____

## The Language of Turtles

I was floating spread-eagle on my back a good distance out from shore in the salty, calm, Gulf of Mexico waters, feeling wind and ocean, sun, and sky. With the water a transparent Caribbean blue, even at that depth I could see straight to the ocean floor, the sparkling white sand reflecting dappled bands of light. I languished, buoyant, enjoying the simplicity of the gorgeous morning, feeling weightless. Suspended between the earth and the sky, my breath rose and fell against the liquid world supporting and surrounding me. Mantra was humming through me like bright fish flashing through the sea. It felt like the mantras were chanting me, rather than me chanting them.

*It felt like the mantras were chanting me,*
*rather than me chanting them.*

I lay adrift on the clear blue waters, a happy mantra girl, floating in my sea of bliss, when suddenly something the size of a human head crested the surface of the shimmering water a few feet away.

My reverie exploded as a sudden blast of wet splattered across me. I was so shocked, so startled, I almost levitated. Sloshing up out of my mantric trance, I turned as an enormous sea turtle turned her patterned, caramel-colored head, looking me straight in the eye. I'm not sure if sea turtles are supposed to be afraid of people, but she simply glanced at me, took a deep, damp breath, and calmly plunged back beneath the ocean surface.

It felt like an invitation, so I dove down after her. Under the water's surface, I found that she held a whole magical ecosystem unto herself, with an array of foot-long black-and-white-striped suckerfish attached to her back and a pod of smaller darting fish shadowing her every move. She was encrusted with barnacles while mossy, dark green seaweed ringed her broad, shell-shingled back. For a while, I followed from a safe distance, watching her fore flippers propel her smoothly through the water, her pointy beak chewing sand.

She was a wild animal, and I didn't know why she was putting up with me.

The mantra was my background song, but the breath was hers. Up and down, breath by breath, we fell into an ancient rhythm of swimming, searching, being. The repetition was calming. She could hold her breath much longer than I, but I matched my breathing rhythm to hers, taking two or three breaths to her one. The mystery of being in her cadence took over and I followed her, then the breath, the mantra, the ocean, and the tide. The rhythm of being, of flowing into her moment felt powerful and primitive. It felt like everything in my world slowed down.

After a while I swam closer, curious, wondering if she would bear me by her magnificent side. She did. We were swimming in sync, and I found myself hovering a bit above her back as she swam out a little deeper. I spread out, floating, star-shaped, to see if I was bigger than her, amazed at her raw beauty. She turned again and with a powerful fin thrust she rose intently, bulleting toward the surface.

Suddenly, her huge body was right beneath me, both of us swimming up, up, up. I couldn't get out of her path fast enough. I yanked my knees to my chest as she shot up past my bare feet, knocking me all akimbo, tumbling upside down behind her tail. Unperturbed—possibly putting me in my place—she swam back down into the oceanic depths once again.

I followed along with her fish posse until I got overexuberant and dove excitedly underneath her pale, leathery belly. That may be a no-no with sea turtles, because she looked down at me and in one great frowning whoosh, she was off, faster and deeper than I could possibly go.

Laughing, I broke the water's surface and turned onto my back, in disbelief at this miraculous encounter. I lay suspended on the water's surface. With sea exhaustion seeping in—the saturation of salt, sun, and sky—I realized we had traveled far together. Repeating my silent mantras, I floundered back to shore, jelly-legged and tired, feeling the radiance of joy, the rhythm of nature coursing through me, one mantra at a time.

### Listening in the Silence

How did this happen? My silence and the mantras seemed to make space for magic. There is a lot of magic in the world, and you may not meet a sea turtle, but what is your magic? Do you pause and make space for it? When we slow down, simplify, and quiet our minds, we remember that we are part of the natural world around us. We connect to the beauty of nature and the simplicity of just being alive. We study ourselves to find our true nature. A yogi is trained to withdraw their senses from the world in order to touch into inner silence. Like a turtle drawing into her shell, we purposefully draw away from stimulus so we can discover who we are without it. Being alone is where we can hear our own voice. No longer obscured by other thoughts and opinions, no longer bombarded with the news, the social media, the constant demand of the world, the mind begins to find a natural rhythm, a cadence.

The more the mind calms down, the more the breaths and mantras can harmonize and organize the energy currents that move through the mind. Suddenly there is so much space. There is so much peace.

*We listen for the silence in between the thoughts.*

We listen for the silence in between the thoughts. We notice the space between the words, between the notes of the songs. We experience the silence in between the breaths. We are being instead of doing. As we practice, listen, and breathe, we merge into yoga—union—developing a comfort, even a resounding, companionship with silence.

## The Art of Breaking Up Together

In the late 1980s, my artist boyfriend was breaking up with me, or we were breaking up together. It's often so hard to tell. Having just returned from a scuba diving trip to the then little-known island of Cozumel, we had agreed I would move out. He would keep the loft. We were breaking apart after cohabitating for a handful of years in a downtown Castleberry Hill artist space. He and I had a good thing; we loved and laughed, explored and created—until we didn't. Both of us were wounded, both figuring out who we were and how we wanted to be in the world. A pile of friends was arriving the next day to help me move, and Tomás and I were arguing over the details.

Tomás had just presented a show of his work at a nearby gallery, rich oil paintings lush with promise, his undeniable talent apparent in every brushstroke. The paintings were all oversized portrayals of a striking German woman named Ruth, a provocative enchantress he claimed he did not have a thing for. I begged to differ.

I didn't believe you could do eight enormous oil paintings of a woman in all stages of undress, her incredibly luminous eyes gazing insolently back at the viewer, without some deeper connection. Or at least some lusty layer of flesh fantasy. But Tomás maintained innocence, and I decided to trust him. But—full truth—I never really trusted her. Or it.

At the end of a long, hot, disgruntling moving day, Tomás showed up with a parting gift: one of the massive paintings of Ruth. I slowly, methodically put on my rose-colored glasses and hung it prominently on my new wall.

### The Other Lover

The real problem lay deeper than Ruth. I was having a love affair of a different ilk, and its name was yoga. I was on a path of radical growth, doing revolutionary personal healing, which I desperately needed and refused to abandon, altering our relationship dynamic. I was fully engaged in the upward climb out of the sewage of my past, and stopping halfway wasn't a choice, not for this intense, longing-for-freedom yogi. Tomás was having a hard time relating and didn't share the same passion for doing powerfully disruptive inner healing. Basically, Tomás and I wanted different things.

A few weeks later, he and I were strolling through my new neighborhood at dusk, returning from a Mexican meal together. We were still dismantling our love relationship, trying to disentangle our hearts and get more honest. Tomás was a quiet, sweet man and I knew him well. He was strung really tight that evening, struggling to convey something, so I was listening, really listening. We walked up the steps and stood at the threshold of my new abode. As I opened the heavy metal door, he put his hand on my arm. I turned back, looking searchingly into his eyes.

"I'm dating Ruth," he stammered.

I took that right through the heart. Dismayed, speechless, I stepped back away from him, across the threshold, and slowly closed the door in his face, with a final definitive thud.

## The Mean Streak

That night I tossed and turned. I raged around the apartment, unable to contain the heartbreak I felt. I attempted to write it out, but my outrage was primal. Words were inaccessible, just out of reach. I felt pure rage with no language, just searing feeling, hot off the emotional press. I violently slapped gesso across a canvas, sloshing much of it onto floor. I stormed back to my sketchbooks, colors in hand, but the images did not express my hatred. I didn't hate Tomás—well, maybe for a minute—but I hated the feeling of being betrayed, of being lied to. In my anguish, I turned and looked at the painting of Ruth.

## The Painting of Ruth's Mustache

Tomás returned the next day. Why we couldn't just pry ourselves apart, I do not know. Breakups are messy, and we were both sticky in it—holding on while letting go. We loved each other, and it was time to move on. He had been in the apartment for five minutes before he noticed the thick, painterly black mustache adorning Ruth's chiseled face.

He leapt from the couch, sped across the room in frantic, panicked strides, and leaned into the painting, panting in hot fast breaths. He asked, "What kind of paint did you use?" I could almost hear his mind clicking away. *Was he more concerned about the damage to his painting than he was to my heart?* I thought.

"What kind of paint did you use?" he demanded, a little louder, a little more desperate, voice quavering. Some of his best work hung on the wall before us, but now, some of mine did as well.

I sauntered up to the painting, reached around him and peeled off the finely crafted sticker I had concocted the night before and then affixed to Ruth's smug face. I pressed it to his soft flannel shirt, right over his heart, looking straight into his eyes. I gave it a soft pat and kept walking.


## The Arrow of Discernment

The night I made the mustache sticker, I used every yogic skill I had not to destroy Tomás's painting. I wanted to reach for a knife or a blowtorch, and both were handily available. I had literally gallons of paint innocently sitting in my new foyer. I talked myself up and then down a number of times. I might have thrown the couch cushions at the painting, viciously and repeatedly. The teachings of svadhyaya, however, demand that we look at ourselves, even when we just want to rage.

The tool I picked up was The Arrow of Discernment, which burdens me with the responsibilities of truth, integrity, and kindness. It instructs me to pull my accusatory finger back to my own chest and let the arrow pierce my own heart. This is not to implicate or shame me. It is to empower me to use everything I experience as fuel for my own evolution.

I, however, was in a raging storm of emotion. I frostily sent the denuded painting home with Tomás, hoping to never lay eyes on it again. Shamefaced, carrying the massive art-work, and churning with words unspoken, he departed. The fabric of heartache was torn further open, ragged edges flapping between us. In order to use this storm to grow, I would need to discern what choice offered real freedom. Together, we chose to step away—no calling, no hanging out, no using each other to bear the aloneness of separation.

The clear boundary was better for both of us. It enabled me to see how holding on and letting go simultaneously was not possible. The Arrow of Discernment asks me to shoot into the battlefield of my own liberation and discern what life is teaching me. Here, I enter the field of accountability, where karmic debts are shed. This reveals a method to learn from my reactions and explore the field of becoming, where I can find who I truly am.

## MINI PRACTICE

### THE ARROW OF DISCERNMENT

When you are caught in a disagreement with someone, have you ever raised your index finger to make a point? Have you slashed your finger around to punctuate your ideas and opinions? This mindfulness tool asks you an essential question: in that moment, can you point the finger back at your own chest as an act of self-discovery?

The Arrow of Discernment teaches us to stand in the eye of the storm, skillfully riding the winds of change. By turning our accusatory finger back to ourselves and aiming true, we find what our reaction is about. We clarify our ability to see and deepen our understanding of ourselves.

The Arrow of Discernment is not a practice in self-flagellation; it is an accountability tool to teach us piercing awareness. Use this tool during arguments and disagreements. Use it when you suspect you were off about something, but don't really want to admit it to yourself. Use it when you get self-righteous. When you are on your high horse. Use it when you are trapped in the desire to be right. Definitely use it when you are mad and can't get unmad.

### The Arrow of Discernment Technique

- If you catch yourself waving your finger to make a vehement point, stop. Slowly draw The Arrow of Discernment (your pointer finger) back to the center of your own chest, your own inner heart, to detect the source of your discord.
- Study your reaction to know yourself.
- With your fingertip on your chest, kindly inquire, "What is my part in this? Have I hurt someone else? Am I hurt by someone else?"
- Ask: "Can I remain in compassionate awareness, share openly, and continue this discussion?"
- Continue the conversation if you can do so with evenness, kindness, and compassion. If not, make a date to do so when you have had the time to discern what has triggered you and how to navigate a path to healing.

## DEEP PRACTICE

### THE MANTRA TO UNTANGLE THE MIND

Is it weird that to quiet the mind, yogis often use mantra? It seems almost contradictory, like using sound to create silence. But understanding how the mind works is one of the biggest keys to the self-study of svadhyaya.

Here's the idea: the human mind thinks all the time, in a constant barrage of endless, repetitive thinking. Some of those thoughts are amazing and some are the same thoughts we experienced yesterday, and the day before. And last week. Last month. Last year. The mind is a tangled creature of habit. We think redundant thoughts on a loop, and the creative clarity of our minds can be obscured by all that mundane repetition. We want a tool to cull out the insightful, innovative thought strands from all the background noise. One of yoga's potent methods to achieve this is mantra, the tool to untangle the mind.

Mantra literally means "mind tool," from the Sanskrit word *manas*, "mind," and *tra*, "tool." Mantras are designed to help practitioners access a higher vibration—the higher mind. Repeating a mantra creates a sense of calm, an unwinding that reveals how incredible our mind is when we are not stressed, anxious, fearful, or angry. By chanting sacred sounds in a vibration-based sacred language like Sanskrit, the restless mind settles into a harmonious rhythm, unified by the repetition. Mantra does not teach us to think no thoughts, which is almost impossible. It teaches us to concentrate on one thought, holding the mind in one-pointed focus. Giving our mind something to focus on other than our thoughts brings relief and unity. Mantra attempts to disentangle, smooth out, and congregate all our random thought strands into a harmonious tapestry, unified by a sacred intention.

*So Ham: The Breath Mantra*

A silent mantra hides inside each breath we take. It is the mantra *So Ham,* pronounced "so-HAHM." It reflects the natural sound of the breath. The inhalation sound is "So," and the exhalation sound is "Ham." In Sanskrit, *so* means "that" and *ham* means "I am." I am that. I am that sacredness, that ultimate reality—that indescribable, untranslatable, universal energy. I am that sacred aliveness. So Ham is the background mantra to every breath we breathe, taken thousands of times each day. It identifies the meditator with the essence of all that exists.

*So Ham Breath Technique*

- Set a timer for five, seven, or ten minutes.
- Sit comfortably for meditation.
- Settle the mind onto the deep, natural rhythm of your breath.
- Begin thinking "So" as you breath in, contemplating "That." You can elongate the sound silently to fill up your mind and resonate over any thoughts.
- Think "Ham" as you breathe out, or "I am."
- Repeat the silent mantra, thinking "So Ham," or "I am that," with each breath. I am that sacred essence, that essential self.
- If your thoughts are dominant, you can silently "shout" the mantra, making it stronger than the thoughts.
- Continue with long deep breaths and settle into a knowing or a befriending of the self.

# 10
# SURRENDERING INTO BLISS

Ishvara Pranidhana: (EESH-vah-dah
prah-nee-DHAN-ah) surrender to
the sacred; devotion

*"Surrender is faith that the power of love can accomplish
anything even when you cannot foresee the outcome."*

DEEPAK CHOPRA

## Shave My Head, Blow My Mind, Pierce My Heart

I was dressed head-to-toe in well-worn white cotton, the glaring Florida sun setting over the palmettos, rain clouds rumbling, drums beating, echoing across the darkening night sky. I was walking into a tantric ceremony where my heavy dark hair would be shorn from my head, an ancient offering and a wild gesture of trust, transformation, and surrender. I would leave changed—not as I had arrived—the outer ceremony reflecting the inner evolution, the remnants of attachment cut away with my hair. I was stepping forward in a traditional but unorthodox lineage that initiates women and LGBTQ people. It's a lineage that tries to be attuned to the spirit of yoga's rich tradition while evolving to include and embrace modern experience, thus expanding beyond any outdated patriarchal views. This monk's initiation was calling forth an inner offering, a giving over of my life in service to humanity, but the spiritual path is unending, the surrender ongoing, the trust tested time and again.

I walked barefoot around the curved arc of the stone ashram path. The sun-soaked stones radiated a comforting warmth against the soles of my bare feet. Hundreds of my own students, as well as devotees of my guru, lined a deep, still pond, all standing, singing, and clapping in anticipation of our arrival. I was surrounded by a jubilant parade of monks, with children darting in and out, all of us feeling the excitement of the night's celebratory vibe. Lights and music glittered across the Ganga Pond, the large body of water named after the holy Ganges River in India where this ritual has been performed since the beginning of time. We processed from shrine to shrine, slowly making our way to the grand proceedings. Garlands of orange marigolds and hot pink carnations bedecked the Neem Karoli Baba Temple, resplendent and awash from a hard summer rain, thunderclouds still looming in the distance. Candlelight and fire, incense and revelry, greeted us from each corner.

This was my *sanyassin* ceremony where I would publicly take vows to become a swami, a revered teacher and leader in the yogic tradition. I felt fully present and calm, held in place by a true inner quiet. I had primed thoroughly for this momentous ritual and felt open, anticipatory, and ready. I felt as if I had been preparing for lifetimes and that one singular breath could crack open the moment, with no doing on my part. I felt like the only thing left to do was surrender, to lift my feet from the warmth of the earth and ride the wave into what was unfolding. I was riding a wave of simple being, a wave of spiritual energy. I moved and bowed, nodded and smiled. I felt deep love more than any other thing. I felt deeply attuned to love.

My guru, Ma, sat on a lush platform beneath a heavy white tent, abundant swags of flowers draped down the sides. More rain was expected, so a cluster of tents, with a mishmash of oversized umbrellas, crowded around the sacred site. I knelt on the rugs laid out before Ma as the ceremony began. The music receded and, as fat raindrops splattered, Ma turned to the head officiant, the *pujari*, the keeper of the fire.

"Begin," she said, and he lifted a ladle of hot melted ghee, pouring the rendered butter over the sizzling flames.

*Agni hotra* is an ancient fire ritual of burning away what we no longer need. It is a ceremonial form of enacted surrender, a relinquishing of negativity. By throwing grains of rice into a consecrated fire while chanting 108 names of the divine feminine, devotees symbolically offer up their attachment, suffering, or illusion. It's a passionate ritual of invoking and releasing that builds in intensity. As the fire is fed, the momentum increases, and the flames dance hotter and higher. As the wood is devoured and transformed into smoke and ash, the offering of our pain is similarly changed and discharged.

The pujari continued chanting the names of the Mother and ladling ghee into the fire. The night sky darkened as the flames leaped. At the pinnacle moment as the priest was bellowing out the last of the sacred names, a rumble rolled across the sky, followed by a large white bird, swooping just overhead. The crowd gasped as the magical fire ritual concluded and the final offering was poured over the blaze.

## Taking the Leap

I turned to Ma as the next phase of the ceremony began. With my thick Irish hair pulled back into a fat ponytail, I reached for both of her hands. Simultaneously, we squeaked out a nervous sound. Ma and I shared a little bit of vanity about having long, beautiful locks. Through these ever-deepening rituals, I was symbolically letting go of my attachments, but this one wasn't easy for either of us. We both took a deep breath. We both lifted our shoulders. We both squeezed tight to each other's hands as the moment of release drew near.

An elegantly tattooed swami, a hairdresser in his day, stepped up behind me and lifted the tail from the nape of my neck, gathering my wayward hair in one hand. With the cool metal scissors alight against my skin, he severed the ponytail from my head in one sharp snick.

Tossing the ponytail to one side, he buzzed a humming electric razor meticulously over my head, lifting random tufts of my shortened hair and shaving all the way down to my scalp. As I reconnected to my breath, I felt a surprising surrender of feminine identity. I might be taking the vows of a swami, but I am a woman, and letting go of all my gorgeous hair had an impact. I felt the inner release, the untangling, the reflexive letting go. The vibrating razor droned back and forth across my scalp, sending shivers tingling up the back of my neck. Suddenly, in one thunderous clap, a hammering downpour of rain began.

Getting to experience the wildness of a full monk's initiation with a living shakti master is a rare opportunity in modern life. This was a shave-off-my-hair, change-my-name, willingly-ask-my-old-identity-to-die kind of experience.

*This was a shave-off-my-hair, change-my-name,*

*willingly-ask-my-old-identity-to-die*

*kind of experience.*

This Vedic ritual is considered a turning point and a recognition of an earnest devotion to the spiritual path. It's a profound commitment, on the level of a spiritual marriage, a ceremonial giving over of one's inner heart. It's an act of turning toward the sacred as the deepest relationship of one's life, a turning over of one's whole being in reverent connection and service to the greater, cosmic good.

In this act, I was going all in, but anyone anywhere can feel the full devotion of their own heart by opening, taking the leap, and loving fully. It's an outrageous act—full-throttle love—because we do it knowing we will be hurt, knowing our hearts will break. Unarmored and courageous, we make an offering of our heart to that which we honor and love. You could love the ocean, the sky, or the Christ. You could bow in adoration to the Buddha or to the present moment. You could offer your whole heart to your partner, your family, or your kids. You could live a life devoted to serving humanity, to catalyzing social justice, to easing suffering, or to living love.

With my head shaved clean, I proceeded with my guru around the edge of the pond. The boisterous crowd stood along the embankment, my sisters solemn next to me, my students and friends observant and intrigued. A clean white cloth was spread on the ground next to a set of wide grassy steps that led down into the murky water of the pond. I lay face down, inhaling the cool damp of the earth beneath me. Ma chanted as she lifted a receptacle of ash, a symbol of purity and of death: death to the ego, death to what limits you, death to who I had been. She poured the ash, in a dusty nebula, over my entire body, anointing me head-to-toe, back to front. Like the sadhus, the yogis of old, I was bald and smothered in ash, and I felt it again, the whisper, the sensation of real surrender. I lay, ashen, with my chest open to the sky. I felt everything and nothing.

Ma placed her left foot on the center of my chest, lifting her right foot off the earth. Standing fully on me, balancing upon my sternum, she cried out, "Om Namah Shivaya," the mantra of liberation. "Om Namah Kali"—my beloved's name was imprinted on my heart forever.

Ma stepped down and, after a moment, I stood slowly, ashy white toes squishing into black mud. I felt ephemeral, both formed and unformed. I looked like a walking corpse, like a dead gray ghost. I waded slowly into the waters of the sacred pond, trail of ash floating, spreading out on the lake's surface behind me like an eerie silhouette, a shadow relic of who I was. I dove under, washing off the past and surrendering the old masks, the old identities, the old everything. I felt the cold cleansing water rinse the powder from my skin. I felt the visceral letting go. I felt the renewal, the awakening of life. Laughing, dunking under, I felt happy and free. I felt the most like me I had ever felt.

After clambering out of the pond, drying off, and stripping naked, my new orange garments seemed strangely vibrant after the monk's whites. After twenty years of abundant devotion on the monk's path, I was a swami now, a higher order of teacher, having made a deeper level of commitment. As we walked back to the Baba Temple, I was vibrating from the inside out, feeling and not quite feeling, pulsing with so much that was new. Ma announced my new names, my titles, and my roles. She painted an ancient tilak, a sacred symbol, atop my bald dome, whispering a Sanskrit mantra in my ear. She pronounced me fit to teach in her name, to carry on the lineage, to be a bearer of light. She challenged me to take up the *vidya*, the wisdom of yoga, and share it out with the world.

To me, it was a proclamation of my surrender. I had let something go, and had experienced a radical, bone-deep release. I had laid it all down, prying my own fingers from clinging too closely to life. I felt the wildness, the sacred energies of the universe holding me, guiding me. I trust that through life and through death, through love and through breath, incredible sacredness holds true. I allow love to course through me, shining from my inner heart like the light of the rising sun breaking across my chest, blazing, fierce, lighting my way forward.

> *I trust that through life and through death,*
> *through love and through breath,*
> *incredible sacredness holds true.*

## Ishvara Pranidhana: Surrender Dorothy

In the West, we have a peculiar distaste for the idea of surrender. As children we learn to fear this concept when "Surrender Dorothy" is scratched jaggedly across the sky in *The Wizard of Oz* by the evil witch, cackling ominously astride her flying broom. The heroes in *Star Trek* teach us to "Never give up. Never surrender." Marvel's *Avengers* declare, "No surrender," as part of their ethos. We think surrender implies defeat—a crushing capitulation. We think it's a submission of power, a bowing down to some bullying influence that now has a dominating, demoralizing supremacy over us.

In yogic belief, however, surrender does not mean giving up; it means letting go. It does not mean giving up power; it means releasing into a more authentic version of it.

Let's say, however, that you long for a love relationship, one that is special and lasting. You make yourself available: you socialize, flirt, and let people know you are looking. You date, peruse the dating apps, and open your heart, but your partner has not shown up, and you have not fallen in love. You start to struggle. Frustration takes over, and you think that to have a romantic partner, you are going to have to *will* them into existence. You begin to despair. How can surrender aid you?

The Indian spiritual teacher Shirdi Sai Baba emphasized patience and faith as part of surrender—the patience to allow things to unfold naturally and the faith that things will happen when the moment is right. I recommend the affirmation "I am not the doer," trusting that the sacred is at play, even when it isn't playing out our way... or at least not yet. This isn't easy because often we just want what we want, or we feel we have been patient enough. Can we surrender our desires to a higher power? Can we have faith when things aren't going our way? What happens if we come to a point where we say to God or the universe: *If you want this to happen, please take care of it, because my way isn't working.* This is a form of surrender. We say, "Let thy will be done." In other words, we keep showing up, we ask for divine assistance, and we trust that it is on its way.

*Ishvara pranidhana implies surrender*
*to a sacred reality,*
*a belief in something bigger than us,*
*some mystical force constantly at play in our lives.*

Ishvara pranidhana implies surrender to a sacred reality, a belief in something bigger than us, a mystical force at play in our lives. Sacred surrender reminds us that we don't know everything. It means we trust in the vastness, the mystery, even the void. It is surrender and devotion to our notion of God. When we surrender, we learn to celebrate the fact that we get to be here, experiencing it all—death and life, misery and joy—as we choose to love anyway.

The first two limbs of yoga's eight-limbed path outline the ten foundations, the yamas and niyamas—the subject of this book. This final guideline is the tenth out of ten for a reason: it does not come easy. Ishvara pranidhana is surrender and devotion to the sacred. To fully comprehend what it means to surrender to the mystical dimensions of life, you'll find it helpful to embody some of the practical wisdom gleaned from the nine earlier principles first.

### After the Ecstasy

After attempting to conquer your inner aggression, release your attachment, train your senses, develop deep concentration, and lean into the resonance of meditation comes the real secret of yoga: bliss. That is the point of all these yogic practices. The bigger secret still? We cannot achieve sustainable bliss without surrender. We need an ongoing relationship with this mysterious, baffling art: the wild wisdom-skill of surrendering to something greater than us. When queried on "Who are we surrendering to?" the Indian guru Bhagawan Nityananda gave the unnervingly brilliant answer: "Surrender to the greatness that is within you."

*"Surrender to the greatness that is within you."*

When we surrender, we taste and experience wholeness to such a degree that we feel good—really good. We feel confident. We back ourselves up. We feel oneness, a profound kinship, with everything and everyone that exists, which creates the foundation for loving community, embodied allyship, and spiritual activism. As *Meditation for the Love of It* author Sally Kempton explains, "Yoga teaches us that there are repeatable experiences of infinite consciousness," and we can surrender to that. We surrender to the ideal that all of us are uniquely valuable and together weave the fabric of a conscious society. If one thread of this colorful tapestry unravels, it pulls against us all. We realize that when we work for the good of one, we influence the collective good. We no longer bow to a hierarchy with a select few on top and the majority of others at the bottom because we know that all of us can obtain and sustain a state of mutual, expansive existence. This involves work—the work of surrendering into love and being loving every day. We do this not just to the people that we are close to, but to those who are challenging or disagreeable. This is the work of embodying ethics and compassion, freedom and truth, over and over again, for all people. We expand our capacity for caring as we surrender into being global citizens.

# MINI PRACTICE

## SURRENDER THE CONTROL FREAK

When we surrender, we learn to celebrate the fact that we get to be here, experiencing it all, whether it's death and life or misery and joy. Life is hopelessly out of our control, but we have the privilege of living it. We can try to force life into submission. We can act powerless or ineffectual. Both these strategies make us less than who we are. But what if we use the yogi's tools of devotion and surrender to enhance and enliven our experience of life?

*Technique*
Sit comfortably for meditation. You can write, speak, or think your answers to the following self-inquiry questions.

Ask yourself:

- Where am I trying to force a situation to be different than it is? Am I exerting excess control with my kids? My partner? My colleagues?

_____

_____

_____

_____

- Sit with your answers for a moment, allowing space to really feel them. Breathe in and out with a sense of allowing, letting yourself acknowledge and feel.

Then ask:

- What am I afraid of?

_____

_____

_____

_____

_____

- What happens if I let go and surrender the illusion of control?

_____

_____

_____

_____

_____

- What do I experience if I surrender into trust and wisdom?

_____

_____

_____

_____

_____

- Sit with your answers again for a moment, allowing space to really feel them as you breathe deeply.

Now ask:

- What am I devoted to?

_____

_____

_____

_____

_____

- What is the difference between devotion and control?

_____

_____

_____

_____

_____

- Sit with your answers again, creating spaciousness to be okay with whatever arises.

End by repeating this three times:

- "I surrender into peace. I am devoted to authentic presence. I am love." Remember that peace, presence, and love are powerful consciousness tools.

## Sliding Up the Wall

I entered my guru's plush living room into a prickly debate. Ma and a close student of hers, an accomplished nurse practitioner, were bickering and I could feel the subtle heat of underlying discord rippling through their exchange.

"I don't. I don't believe you could do that. I don't even know if I think it's a real thing," said the healthcare worker, definitively.

Surrounded by oversized statues, paintings, crucifixes and icons from every possible faith tradition, the dark room was thick with sacred splendor, a reverent floor to ceiling collection of diverse, divine imagery. Ma, however, was fully focused on this discussion. The two of them were obviously taking opposing views, but I didn't know the topic. And truth be told, I didn't really care. I was distracted. I was preparing for an afternoon session where Ma was teaching spiritual philosophy, then leading a meditation. Dozens of my own students were attending, and many of them were having their own conflicts. I was busy ruminating over their issues, sorting them all out in my head.

I didn't have the bandwidth for another clash, so I tuned their conversation out. With a messy pile of notes in one hand, I hitched up my draped silk top with my other hand and slid down a nearby wall, sitting inconspicuously off to one side. Patiently half-listening, I was hoping they would resolve this matter on their own.

The argumentative blond practitioner continued her provocative jabbing: "Why would I? Why would anyone? I don't even know if levitation is a real thing. And even if I did... no, I don't think you could make me levitate."

Mm-hmm, this was the conflict. You really cannot make this stuff up. They parried back and forth a few more times while I organized my papers. I was not really paying attention to an exchange that held little impact for me—or so I thought.

After a few more moments, we gathered our things and collectively traversed out to the meditation hall. Unceremoniously, I took my typical seat on the wood floor close to Ma with my back against the wall and my legs folded beneath me. I tucked myself meticulously onto my zafu cushion to ward off the meditator's plague of falling-asleep legs. I sat tall, listened attentively, and took notes as Ma began to teach. The room was thick with shakti, or spiritual energy, and I felt the soft inner hum of bliss rising within me. Ma began teaching about an energetic space at the base of the spine that was tightly closed like a plug blocking a drain. I had often heard her teach about the first chakra, about kundalini uncoiling, and about unraveling our karmic knots. Today, however, the discourse held something unique, some intriguing bit of newness that tickled my mind, awakening a deep but uncomplicated curiosity.

## The Beckoning of the Cosmos

To begin the meditation, Ma invited us all to close our eyes. Rolling the weight forward on my hips, I sat with the curve of my lower back arched gently, my chest lifted, and my shoulders soft. I could hear Ma's voice guiding us, directing me further into my inner experience. After three or four minutes—a short amount of time for these intense meditation sessions—I suddenly felt a subtle pop, a funny, unfamiliar sensation at the base of my spine, almost like a soda can opening, only on the inside, releasing pressure. I felt air, space, and openness.

From my lowest spine something burst open and everything... lifted up. I felt the wall ripple behind me. I was buoyant, experiencing a lightness of form, a total silence, and an absolute absence of thought. Something clicked into place—like the tumblers of the universe aligning—and as energy surged up my spine, I was irrefutably in the deepest meditation of my life, imperceptibly sliding up the wall. I was encompassed in ecstasy, the silence astounding, the quiet filled with illumination. I entered a dazzling, mesmerizing expansion of light. I sensed the easing away, the dissolution of my physical form, my body inconsequential, like ash dispersing effortlessly into the wind. I experienced a profound release from reality, a crumbling of attachment, and a thorough embodiment of relief.

Wrapped inside a beckoning from the cosmos, I was held like a lover, by the beloved. I do not know if I levitated, but I understood with full comprehension why people thought they did. Bliss and ecstasy had their way with me for the duration of the meditation—maybe thirty or forty minutes, maybe thirty or forty lifetimes. I surrendered to all that was occurring and experienced timelessness as one breath, one moment that lasted forever. I experienced the merge, no separation between who I was and who was the universe, who was consciousness and who was all that exists. This is the *yuj*, the yoke, the union with the sacred. I experienced yoga, right when carelessly I wasn't expecting to experience anything at all.

### The Quiet Internal Waves

At the conclusion of the practice, Ma led us back down to the base of the spine, and I felt as if the very matter of my body, my cellular structure, coalesced back into shape, reoccupying the form of my body. It was like I dissolved and reformed, and it felt as natural as breathing. As I opened my eyes, I was amazed to see the room just as it was, my body still the same, my legs still hovering on the edge of sleep. I felt amazing, laughing, lit from the inside. I hefted my heavy legs, hugging my knees to my chest and running my hands over my own form to reassure myself I was still here.

Riding on a breath of being, I stood on unsteady limbs as Ma, ever raucous, ever intense, ever joyful, left the room, calling out to the goddess as she departed. I rotated, in amazement, slowly looking around, absorbing the richness.

Taking a tenuous step, then weaving through the crowd, I entered a happy sea of humanity. I drifted over to connect with a cluster of my students, curious to see what they felt and what they had experienced. I rode the quiet internal waves, feeling deeply aware—both internally and externally—and surrendered, merged into everyday bliss.

## That Cranky Limiting Mind

In a recent chat with spiritual teacher and author of *Dream,* Marcia Wieder, she explained, "We often believe that mastery takes ten thousand hours of practice, but it's possible—just like with enlightenment—to have it occur in a moment." I wasn't sure how that incredible moment occurred. How did those tumblers click into place? How did that pop and lift happen? I wanted to repeat it again, frequently, because, you know: more meditative ecstasy, simple and silent bliss, embodied and relentless love. We all want more of that, right? Yoga is union with that state of grace, that total oneness. If that monumental meditation was real yoga, I wanted to experience more of it, immediately. Over decades of daily meditation, I have learned not to get attached to the "bells and whistles" of practice, but this was phenomenal. All meditators reluctantly learn that some days you have mind-blowing experiences and some days you listen to the endless, cranky, judgmental, monkey-jumping mind.

During this experience, however, I was with my guru, a living tantric master. So, later that evening, I wrote her, sharing my experience and asking for input or guidance. I would see Ma the next day and was aware that she loved answering queries in person.

The following afternoon, when we were all nestled in around her for another teaching-and-meditation session, Ma commented on my experience. She explained that a belief in something greater than us keeps our mind flexible and open—in her words, juicy. Ma shared that when we stop paying so much attention to our thoughts, a gap opens in between the thoughts where real mystery comes alive. Then she playfully told the story of me and the healthcare worker. The one who contested the mysticism couldn't quite get it; meanwhile, the one who didn't even think about it, slipped right in. She spoke about the process of trust, faith, and surrender as keys to transcending the limited mind.

*She spoke about the process of trust, faith, and surrender as keys to transcending the limited mind.*

I benefitted from the healthcare worker's snarky throwdown. I mean, she was challenging a Brooklyn guru, questioning her ability, and Ma was a true shakti teacher. Ma embodied an outrageous amount of spiritual energy and could blast you awake in a Kali-esque, sword-swinging, hang-on-to-your-head manner.

Each one of us has the innate ability to taste that incredible quiet when we meditate consistently. Surrender is part of accessing that state, and surrender is multifaceted and nuanced. It is difficult to attain without a deft teacher. Surrender asks us to trust something outside ourselves, a wild unknown, a sacred reality at play in the universe. It asks us to remember the evolution of each one of us is relevant, because none of us is free until all of us are free. A teacher is incredibly helpful because we don't know what we don't know. We can't surrender what we can't see, and most often we can only see ourselves from our own point of view. A teacher can look at us objectively and point out things we can't perceive or don't want revealed. If we can surrender to that, watch out! Transformation is on its way. Bliss and ecstasy are right there, hidden just around that next meditative corner, patiently and luminously waiting for us.

## DEEP PRACTICE

### DISSOLVING MEDITATION

This meditation can create a wild experience of surrender. It is an advanced method to explore who you are beyond your body, without your human form. It invites you to surrender into spirit. Here, we climb the path of the chakras: the energy centers along the spine, then overhead into the formless essence of the atman, the soul-self. We also use the five natural elements that compose everything in existence—earth, water, fire, air, and space—to deepen our experience. This is a transcendental meditation because you transcend the body. You must enlist the power of your creative imagination along with curiosity about chakras and the subtle body to immerse fully into this practice.

*Dissolving Meditation Technique*

I recommend recording your own voice reading the following meditation or following the version on my website at www.swamijayadevi.com. This is a longer meditation practice, so following along with a guided recording will be easier.

Sit in a comfortable posture for meditation. Close your eyes. Deepen your breath and begin to relax. Continue deep breathing, releasing the demands of your daily life until you feel calm, centered, and present. This may take three or 103 breaths; just be patient and listen for when you are ready to dive deeper. Continue very long deep breaths throughout the meditation.

Focus at the base of your spine, the root chakra, feeling stable and settled. This is the home of kundalini, the coiled energy of potential transformation. Allow yourself a moment to lovingly feel the solidity of your physical form, your temple-home throughout this life. Then, imagine that the base of your spine, your legs, and feet begin to safely and softly dissolve, like a sandcastle slowly crumbling back into the ocean. Imagine earth returning to earth, like ash, mud, and bone. Feel the physical substance of your body, with your legs dissolving, heavy and empty at the same time. The first chakra dissolves into the first element, earth.

Move your focus up the spine to the second chakra, just above the pubic bone, deep inside your lower abdomen. Feel your hips, pelvis, and sacrum dissolving into water, rushing like rivers pouring through your lower body. You feel the origin of the rivers originating from the four cardinal directions, yourself held gently within their flow. With water gushing, the five elements expressed in the body begin to return to their natural form. The second chakra dissolves into water, as the fluid essence of the creative impulse flows.

Like the sun rising up the dissolving spine, sunlight glinting off the river, a fire in the belly is lit. The third chakra is alight with fire, consumed by the sun, merging fire into fire and light into light. The earthly body combusts, disperses, and heals as personal power is ignited, flames leap, and sunlight shines through. The physical definition of form is loosened further—earth, then water, then fire—and consumed in the smoke and ash rising from the radiant belly fire infusing the solar plexus. The five natural elements are at home in the chakras.

Like flames dancing ever upward, you follow the fire to the center of the chest, the heart chakra—the heart of your very being. In this space, you are expansive and open, soft, strong, and free. Air and wind uplift you as your hands and arms become ephemeral; your ribcage, chest, and spine disperse into air. The wind of the breath takes the dissolution of the body up, like smoke rising from the sacred inner fire, and you trust as the heart chakra becomes like air.

Exhale any constriction at the throat chakra and feel the four sides of the throat creating an energetic container of space. Expand that space, breath by breath, until the throat is clear and open. The breath becomes louder in the throat, then softer, louder, then softer. Feel spacious. Feel vast. Exhale anything clouding this spacious reality. Begin to wonder who you are beyond your body as the throat chakra creates and becomes space.

Focus just between the eyebrows, the mystical place of the third eye, the home of intuition. Hold your focus powerfully at this focal point and feel awareness rising through your whole shadow-body, as the outline of your corporal form dissolves, relinquishing its tight hold. Inside the indistinct outline of your physical form, you begin to see the soft darkness of the night sky. The planets are slowly revealed behind the chakras as you merge with the universe itself. The field of what you were begins to clear the history of many lifetimes, bringing you into the dissolving reality of the now. You are and you are not. You know you have touched this depth before because you are this depth.

Move your focus to the point at the top of the head, where the baby soft spot was when you were an infant. Imagine this crowning point, holding your attention to this place, aligning your soul to this space in time. Ask wisdom to influence your moment as you feel the passage of time, breath by breath, then heartbeat by heartbeat. You perceive that you will outlast your body. You clearly comprehend that you are not limited by this form. You touch into the soul-body, the self that does not die at death.

Draw your awareness up through the top of the head as the ash-of-what-was falls gently to the earth and you are released. You are free. Remain aware of the space just over the head, the sky of consciousness. You are that sky. You are that consciousness. You are the purity of spirit, the essence of the soul. You are being and non-being, form and formless combined. Ride the wind of the breath into the essence of simple being.

After some time, notice the mind, ever restless, ever active. Through awareness of your breath, find a stillness, an ability to focus beyond the restless thoughts. Look for the space between the thoughts. Now go higher—way up over the head into the emptiness. The soul knows no bounds, and you are the soul. Give yourself over to know that you are capable of a deep, focused moment.

Dissolving into the sky of awareness, you are undefined and free. Surrender into the greatness of who you are without form. Vow to love every moment here on earth, to embody love, to love anyway. Know that you are made up of love, and to love you ultimately return.

Slowly, come back to the form of your body, the top of your skull, the crown of your head. Take a deep breath, and breathe your way back into the moment, back into your earthly form, into embodiment. Breathe the universe in through the skull because you are the universe. Hold the breath. Travel down to the heart chakra, the center of the chest. Breathe out, and let the cosmos fill your heart, expanding your capacity to love. Love everything and love everyone because to dissolve into freedom, we must love all of it. The heart dissolves into pure love, infusing the whole of your being and the whole of the universe.

Take a deep breath in with a strong sound. As you release the breath, gently open your eyes. Touch your body and thank it for holding you. Trust you are just as you should be, your form as your ally, flaws and all. As you breathe in trust and surrender, know that everything is working out, that you are always learning, that life is forming and unforming, inside and all around you. Know that you are loved, and you are love. You are consciousness, embodied.

# CONCLUSION
# EMBODIMENT

*"Love is the strongest medicine. It is more powerful than electricity."*

NEEM KAROLI BABA

## Embodying What Is

Writing this book during the COVID-19 quarantine was a labor of love—and self-love. Like so many of us, I was alone, frightened, and uncertain. I leaned into the practices outlined in this book more than I ever have before. In the past, when I would deepen into practice, I would most often approach it from curiosity and exploration: How does this practice change me? Can I use this suffering as fuel to grow?

Can I feel love and connection to my sacred source? Where is the space between my thoughts and do I experience vastness there? What is the silence teaching me?

The coronavirus lockdown, however, altered something in me. I felt my intentional aloneness acutely. When I feel something deeply, I attempt to get quiet and listen to it. Even though we had moved our yoga and meditation community to an online platform, I missed being in a thriving spiritual community. I missed my people, my satsang, and my fellow yogis. I missed everyday camaraderie. I decided to use the feeling of this quarantine, which for me was one of contraction, to expand my creativity. This is yoga, the union of opposites. Similar to my create-to-destroy tactic in The Eggs of Rage story, I used the destruction of COVID-19 to create this body of work.

The writing process inspired me to free myself from more things that were holding me back. Sharing the stories in this book took me to a deeper level of vulnerability, and I believe that vulnerability and realness set us free. I hope this book inspires you to free yourself and live the life you want to live, because this is a book about freedom.

## Heal Yourself to Heal the World

The Ten Tools of Transformation outlined in this book describe a lived experience. They facilitate a moment-by-moment awareness, a breath-by-breath caring that we—and society—desperately need. The world we have created requires an authenticity makeover. However, each of us sits at the heart of this momentous change—because to heal the world we have to heal ourselves. We must choose to do our personal evolutionary work.

In the Introduction, we started with some self-reflective questions. How would you answer the following questions after reading this book?

- Who do I want to be?

- What do I need to do to become that person?

- Which of these tools will help me become the version of myself I envision?

- Which practice or tool will I choose to use first?

## Spiritual Activism

As a spiritual activist, I rely on the sacred. The demand is high on caregivers and spiritual people—anyone trying to nurture the world into being a more equitable, loving place. To believe in the good, we need to remain connected to the good. As my guru said, we must learn to "drink as we pour." We must use tools to forge an unshakable connection to sacred awareness, so we do not burn out. We practice filling our cup every day, allowing the sacred to flow through us, to touch us and fill us. The wisdom energies of the universe are constantly reaching toward us, pouring love into us, aiding us in our liberation, supporting our freedom quest. Will we turn toward them? We ask ourselves:

- Is my cup full?

- In this moment, how connected am I to the sacred?

- Am I a co-creator with sacred reality?

- Can I breathe in a deeper moment?

- What small, consistent practice will I do to fill my cup?

- Is my kindness lived?

When we trust in the essence of all that exists, we embody the essence of being. We trust that at all times—whether we are struggling with a conflict, immersed in meditation, or just being in a simple moment—our voice, our sense of self, is empowered by practice. We are forever in the process of being and becoming, being and becoming, as we do the gratifying work of amplifying our awareness and our ability to love.

## Everyday Liberation

The *Bhagavad Gita* claims "yoga is skill in action." This skill-fulness calls to mind the fluidity of a marital artist, moving with a strike instead of against it, like in *The Matrix*. That nimble action is a way of embodying wisdom, because it hurts a lot more when you bludgeon yourself directly back against a blow. We want to dance with life, rolling with the hits instead of railing against them. Skillful action teaches us to use the force of our own suffering to move more fully into being.

*Skillful action teaches us*
*to use the force of our own suffering*
*to move more fully into being.*

Yogis aspire to use these skills to embody love and authentic freedom. This can be called nirvana, bliss, joy, or even liberation. Liberation sounds lofty—even unattainable—but its essence is simple: liberation from the thoughts and acts that bind us to suffering. It's not that we won't suffer; of course we will—we all do. But we realize that a deeper truth exists within that is quietly waiting beyond the suffering. Awareness of this deeper self liberates us. It unshackles us from unhealed trauma and places us at the eye of the storm of our life. Here, we can stand with our inner heart open. We can be strong. We can love anyway. Here, we are daring enough to become wildly, passionately, full-throttle, hair-blowing-back, get-the-hell-out-of-my-way free.

## Embody the Sacred Beloved

Through all our experiences—from the craziest to the most mundane—we seek wholeness. Yet the wholeness we seek is the wholeness of coming home, of coming back to ourselves.

We want to feel at home in our bodies, to cherish our flesh, our physical form, and to be kind to ourselves. We want to be grateful that we get to be here, to be alive and experience it all—the heartbreak and the joy—because in our bodies we can evolve in ways that are otherwise not possible. We want to care for our body like the sacred beloved it is.

We want to be at home in our hearts, to allow heartache to break us open to love more, instead of just breaking us. We want to soften and make ourselves vulnerable to love. We want to be bold enough to share ourselves with those around us, to be flawed and evolving even when it's hard. We want to care for our heart like the sacred beloved it is.

We want to feel at home in the world, amidst the chaos of modern society. We want to embrace the humanity of each individual. We want our curiosity to fuel our compassion. We may not always understand or agree with the world the way it is, but it is our home. We want to care for the earth like the sacred beloved it is.

If yoga is union, it is this drawing together, this cohesion, this reimagining, that creates wholeness. It is the wholeness of embodying ourselves as home. It is homecoming. It is creating a society of sacred beloveds—nurturing ourselves, our neighbors, our communities, and our planet—while we love our way into wholeness for ourselves.

You are not here to live anyone else's life. You are here to live yours, in holy union—alive and vibrant—experiencing it all, loving anyway.

Embody the whole of your experience. Embody reality. Embody the moment, so that over and over again, you embody love.

# THE TEN TOOLS FOR TRANSFORMATION

These are the ten guidelines outlined in *Patanjali's Yoga Sutra* as the yamas and niyamas. Here I share the traditional definition and my lived experience.

- **Ahimsa:** (uh-HIM-suh)
  Traditional definition: nonviolence; non-harming
  Lived definition: embodied peace
- **Satya:** (SUHT-yah)
  Traditional definition: truth
  Lived definition: embodied truth
- **Asteya:** (uhh-STAY-uh)
  Traditional definition: non-stealing
  Lived definition: embodied self-worth
- **Brahmacharya:** (bruhm-HUH-char-yuh)
  Traditional definition: wise use of energy, to walk with the sacred
  Lived definition: embodied wisdom
- **Aparigraha:** (uh-PAR-EE-grah-HAH)
  Traditional definition: detachment, non-greediness
  Lived definition: embodied love
- **Saucha:** (SOW-chuh)
  Traditional definition: purity, cleanliness, holiness, simplicity
  Lived definition: embodied sacredness

- **Tapas:** (tuh-puhs)
  Traditional definition: discipline, to generate heat and light
  Lived definition: embodied transformation
- **Santosha:** (sahn-TOW-shuh)
  Traditional definition: contentment, equanimity
  Lived definition: embodied well-being
- **Svadhyaya:** (svahd-YAI-yuh)
  Traditional definition: self-study, introspection, contemplation
  Lived definition: embodied presence
- **Ishvara Pranidhana:** (EESH-vah-dah prah-nee-DHAN-ah)
  Traditional definition: surrender to the sacred, devotion
  Lived definition: embodied awareness

# GLOSSARY OF YOGIC TERMS

Most of these yogic terms are in Sanskrit, the primary language of yoga.

- *Acharya* Revered teacher.
- *Agni* Fire; one of the five elements that make up the material universe.
- *Agni Hotra* Vedic fire ritual where ghee (melted clarified butter) is ladled into a consecrated fire to ignite transformation.
- *Ahimsa* Nonviolence, non-harming. The first of the five yamas.
- *Aparigraha* Detachment, non-possessiveness. The fifth of the five yamas.
- *Asana* Yoga posture, the physical poses of yoga.
- *Ashram* Holy sanctuary; often includes residences for the guru and her students.
- *Asteya* Non-stealing. The third of the five yamas.
- *Atman* Universal soul or self.
- *Bhagavad Gita* Song of God. An essential yogic text outlining the major paths of yoga.
- *Bhakti* Devotion and love for the sacred.
- *Bhakti Yoga* One of four major yogic paths outlined in the *Bhagavad Gita*; a path to union with the sacred through love and devotion.

- *Bhastrika* Bellows; a form of yogic breath to ignite the fire of transformation within.
- *Brahmacharya* To walk with God; conservation and intentional use of energy. The fourth of the five yamas.
- *Chakra* Wheel; an energy center within the subtle body with seven major chakras along the spinal column correlating with the nervous system.
- *Chandra* Moon.
- *Darshan* The grace of seeing a guru or holy person and receiving their teaching.
- *Dharana* Meditative focus or concentration; the sixth of the eight limbed path of yoga.
- *Dhuni* Consecrated fire pit, symbolizing the fire within where we burn suffering as fuel to grow.
- *Dhyana* Meditation; the seventh of the eight limbed path of yoga.
- *Ego* In yoga, the individuals I-ness, the sense of self that identifies with the body, mind, and senses.
- *Ganga* The sacred Ganges River in India; recognized as a life-giving, liquid form of the Goddess.
- *Ghat* The steps descending into the Ganges River or other river in India.
- *Guru* A being with great spiritual mastery who is able to ignite and guide students into the highest states of awareness.
- *Gurubai* Students of the same spiritual teacher.
- *Ishta Devata* Personal form of the sacred that resonates most for you.
- *Ishvara Pranidhana* Surrender, devotion. The fifth of the five niyamas.
- *Kali* Tantric Black goddess who slays devotees' egos to catalyze their liberation.

- **Karma** Cause and effect; reaction; karma binds us to the earth, caught involuntarily in the cycle of life, death, and rebirth.
- **Karma Yoga** Seva; one of four major yogic paths outlined in the *Bhagavad Gita*; a path of selfless service.
- **Kashi** Holy city of the yogis in India also called Varanasi or Benares.
- **Kirtan** Devotional singing, most often in Sanskrit.
- **Kundalini** Supreme power of awareness, primordial shakti; the raw, coiled life force at the base of the spine, waiting to be awakening through spiritual practice to clear the energetic path to bliss.
- **Mala** Garland.
- **Mantra** Mind tool; a sacred word, syllable or phrase repeated to focus the mind, aid meditation and access spiritual wisdom.
- **Mauna** Silence; not speaking to enhance the silence of the mind; intentional peace of mind created by periods of silence.
- **Meditation** The state of mind when you are in union, or yoga, and the fluctuations of your mind cease; quiet contemplation.
- **Mudra** A gesture or seal to invoke and express inner consciousness.
- **Namah** Salutations to.
- **Namaste** An honorific greeting; the soul in me honors the soul in you.
- **Niyama** An observance or guideline for living a yogic life; five tools for transformation; the second limb of Patanjali's Eight Limbed Path of Yoga.
- **Om** Or aum; the primordial sound form, the sacred sound of the universe; the vibration of consciousness.

- *Patanjali* A sage in ancient India; the author/compiler of the Yoga Sutra.
- *Prana* The life force, the vital essence of life, energy; linked with but not limited by the breath.
- *Pranayama* Yogic breath control; a system of techniques to harness and manipulate energy.
- *Pratyahara* Withdrawal of the senses; the fifth of Patanjali's Eight Limbed Path of Yoga.
- *Pujari* A vedic or tantric practitioner who performs sacred rituals and ceremonies called pujas.
- *Rishi* A seer or sage who has discovered universal truths through periods of deep meditation.
- *Sadhana* Daily spiritual practice.
- *Sadhu* A holy person, yogi, or monk; one who keenly does *sadhana*, the practices of yoga.
- *Samadhi* Sustained absorption in bliss; the state in which the individual soul and the universal soul unite; ecstatic oneness with the sacred; the eighth of Patanjali's Eight Limbed Path of Yoga.
- *Sankalpa* A spiritual intention.
- *Sanskrit* The classical literary language of India. It is a language based in vibration.
- *Santosha* Contentment, equanimity, being at ease. The third of the five niyamas.
- *Sanyassin* One who lays it all down, a renunciate or monk.
- *Satya* Truth. The second of the five yamas.
- *Saucha* Purity, cleanliness, simplicity. The first of the five niyamas.
- *Seva* Selfless service, giving without looking to see who is taking.
- *Shakti* The divine feminine energy of awakening; kundalini + love = shakti.

- **Shiva** The king of the yogis; the divine masculine energy; absolute reality.
- **Sushumna** Central grace-filled channel of energy in the body that runs from the base of the spine to the top of the head.
- **Sutra** Thread of wisdom.
- **Svadyaya** Self-study, introspection, contemplation. The fourth of the niyamas.
- **Swami** A spiritual teacher or leader; a pundit.
- **Tantra** Continuous; a mystical path of yoga and series of esoteric practices that uses every experience in life as an opportunity to evolve and unite with consciousness.
- **Tapas** Discipline or austerity. The second of the five niyamas.
- **Tilak** A sacred mark anointed on the forehead.
- **Upanishads** The ancient teachings of the forest sages in India, espousing oneness with the sacred.
- **Vipassana** An ancient mindfulness meditation technique of observing the mind without reaction.
- **Yantra** A geometric image or artistic representation, used to direct sacred energy and sometimes as an object of meditation.
- **Yama** An observance, restraint or guideline for living a yogic life; five tools for transformation; the first limb of Patanjali's Eight Limbed Path of Yoga.
- **Yoga** Union, wholeness, yoking to the sacred; spiritual disciplines leading to oneness.
- **Yoga Sutra** A collection of yogic texts collated or written by the sage Patanjali.
- **Yuj** To join, yoke, or unite; the root syllable of the word yoga.

# ACKNOWLEDGMENTS

It took an entire community of beloveds to complete this book. I am overwhelmed with gratitude for all of you.

The deepest respect and gratitude to:

My editors: Swami Jaya Das Murphy, Regina Stribling, Kaity Van Riper, Shawna Quigley.

My beta readers: Martha Scherzer, Shanti Sanchez, Rich Merritt, Tammie Mobley, Katie Pontious, Shakiyla Smith, Marc Pimsler, Jaya Reinhalter, Mary Donovan, Martha Lampella, Swami Mata Giri.

My author allies: Dr. Sue Morter, Lama Rod Owens, Dr. Chelsea Jackson Roberts, Maya Marcia Weider, Dr. John Douillard, and Devadatta David Nelson. Thank you also to Susanna Barkataki, Daniel Simpson, Rick Wright, Jacoby Ballard, and Sally Kempton.

My cover designer: Professor Annika Kappenstein.

My publisher: Eric Koester, Creator Institute, New Degree Press, Georgetown University.

The most soothing reading voice ever: Michael Arendt.

And the deepest thanks to my early supporters. You believed in me before this book was fully born:

Aaron Haefle

Abby + Bre Gaskins

Ainsley Waken

Alex Curtis

Alex Zinnes

Alexa Brewster

Alexandra Walker

Alison Hastings

Allison Bernal

Allison Parker

Allison Summers

Amanda Parramore

Amy Fasula

Annie Padnuk

Annika Kappenstein

Arielle Conway

Ashley Clifton

Betty Milton

Blake Ivey

Brad Fenwick

Brawner Raymond

Carol Sue Young

Carole Cohen

Carrie Keane

Cathy Huyghe

Charisse M. Williams

Charlotte Starfire

Chesley Flannery

Chinnamasta Stiles

Chrissy Diamond

Christina Colangelo

Christine Newcombe

Christine Ryall

Christy Sasser

Collen Beard

Dharmaki Wiser

Dr. Chelsea Jackson Roberts

Dr. Melissa Kulick

Elaine Agnes

Elisabeth Brodie

Elizabeth Isom

Elizabeth Musick

Emily Christianson

Eric Koester

Eve + David Haeseler

Ganesh Lee

Gerald Mitchell

Heather Havey

Ian Campbell

Ilya Levtin

Ismay Campbell

Jamie Fergerson

Jane Weir

Janina Edwards

Jason Rudra Brumbelow

Jaya Reinhalter

Jessica Lam

Joanne Falke

Jon Rosenthal
Joy Dillard Appel
Kasey Cromer
Katie Pontious
Katie Scheibel
Kellie McDonald
Kelly Lions
Kim Alford
Kryz Khaewkhum
Kwang Mae Cho
Kyala Ahava
Lauren West
Linda Lazarri
Lindsey Reynolds
Lisa Fasana
Lisa Vasatka
Liz Kali Marvel
Lynn Serrato
Mahatara Nierman
Marc Pimsler
Marie Timmel
Margot Meeker
Martha Lampella
Martha Scherzer
Mary Donovan
Mary Ellen Greenberg
Mary Hinely
Mary Kate Hewes
Maureen Haley
Melissa Burnett
Melissa Quist
Melissa Shine

Meredith Stocking
Michael Arendt
Michael R. Forrester
Michelle LaCombe
Mike Oxford
Miriam E. Phields
Mowry McClure-Maldonado
Neda Honarvar
Neelam Patel
Nickie Medici
Pam Ahern
Polly Maliongas
Rachel Wellborn
Rachel Wittenberg
Rachel Zick
Richard Dew
Richard W. Merritt
Rick Wright
Robert Butler
Ruby Jordan
Saivite Wilson
Sandy Stovall
Sara Maffey
Satu Sullivan
Scott Patterson
Scott Turner Schofield
Sean Owen
Shakiyla Smith
Shannon McLendon
Shantel Roark
Shanti Sanchez
Shavonna Warthen

Spencer + Hunter Pierce
Stephanie Jones
Susan Voelker
Swami Agni Ma
Swami Jaya Das
Swami Krishnabai
Swami Rudra Das
Tammie Mobley
Tanya Farshi

Tikva Kingrea
Tony Conway
Vicki Golay
Vicky Walker
Victoria Cassity
Violet Conway
William Ty Bittner
Yolonda L. Cameron

# APPENDIX

## Chapter One

Doyle, Glennon. *Untamed.* New York: The Dial Press, 2020.

Hill, Evan. "How George Floyd Was Killed in Police Custody." *New York Times,* May 31, 2020. https://www.nytimes.com/2020/05/31/us/george-floyd-investigation.html.

## Chapter Two

Einstein, Albert. "My Number One Tip for Solving Problems" Debbie Woodbury. *HuffPost,* May 2, 2013. https://www.huffpost.com/entry/problem-solving-advice_b_3185536.

## Chapter Three

Brown, Brené. "Brené Brown and Oprah on Guilt and Shame." Oprah.com. *Super Soul Sunday,* October 18, 2019. Video 0:27. https://www.oprah.com/own-super-soul-sunday/dr-brene-brown-why-guilt-is-better-than-shame-video.

Guatama, Siddhartha. "The Four Noble Truths." *BBC,* November 17, 2009. https://www.bbc.co.uk/religion/religions/buddhism/beliefs/fournobletruths_1.shtml.

## Chapter Four

Griswold, Eliza. "Yoga Reconsiders the Role of the Guru in the Age of #MeToo." *The New Yorker,* July 23, 2019. https://www.newyorker.com/news/news-desk/yoga-reconsiders-the-role-of-the-guru-in-the-age-of-metoo.

World Health Organization. "Devastatingly Pervasive: 1 in 3 Women Globally Experience Violence." Joint News Release. March 9, 2021. https://www.who.int/news/item/09-03-2021-devastatingly-pervasive-1-in-3-women-globally-experience-violence.

## Chapter Five

Bhagavad Gita excerpt from *The Enlightened Heart: An Anthology of Sacred Poetry.* Translated by Stephen Mitchell. New York: Harper Perennial, 1989.

Katha Upanishad. From *The Upanishads* translated by Eknath Easwaran. Berkeley, CA: Nilgiri Press, 1987.

## Chapter Six

Hahn, Thich Nhat. *No Mud, No Lotus: The Art of Transforming Suffering.* Berkeley, CA: Parallax Press, 2014.

Harris, Gardiner. "Cities in India Among the Most Polluted, W.H.O. Says." *New York Times,* May 8, 2014. https://www.nytimes.com/2014/05/09/world/asia/cities-in-india-among-the-most-polluted-who-says.html.

## Chapter Eight

Bhagavad Gita. From The *Bhagavad Gita* translated by Eknath Easwaran. Berkeley: Nilgiri Press, 1985.

Chowdhury, Madhuleena. From "The Neuroscience of Gratitude and How It Affects Anxiety and Grief." PositivePsychology.com. May 2, 2022. https://positivepsychology.com/neuroscience-of-gratitude.

Seligman, Steen, Park, & Peterson. From *"Positive Psychology Progress: Empirical Validation of Interventions."* American Psychologist. Rhode Island, 2005. https://www.researchgate.net/publication/7701091_Positive_Psychology_Progress_Empirical_Validation_of_Interventions.

## Chapter Nine

The Yoga Sutra of Patanjali translated by Edwin F. Bryant. New York: North Point Press, 2009.

Bhagavad Gita. From The *Bhagavad Gita* translated by Eknath Easwaran. Berkeley: Nilgiri Press, 1985.

## Chapter Ten

Nityananda, Bhagawan. From "Morning Pujas and Prayers." *The Teachings of Ma Jaya Sati Bhagavati* (blog). October 27, 2017. https://www.kashi.org.

## Conclusion

Bhagavad Gita. From The *Bhagavad Gita* translated by Eknath Easwaran. Berkeley: Nilgiri Press, 1985.